Augustus Craven, Georgiana Fullerton

Natalie Narischkin

Sister Of Charity Of St. Vincent Of Paul, Volume 2

Augustus Craven, Georgiana Fullerton

Natalie Narischkin
Sister Of Charity Of St. Vincent Of Paul, Volume 2

ISBN/EAN: 9783337300364

Printed in Europe, USA, Canada, Australia, Japan

Cover: Foto ©Lupo / pixelio.de

More available books at **www.hansebooks.com**

NATALIE NARISCHKIN

Sister of Charity of St. Vincent of Paul

BY

Mrs. AUGUSTUS CRAVEN

AUTHOR OF "A SISTER'S STORY"

TRANSLATED BY

LADY GEORGIANA FULLERTON

IN TWO VOLUMES.—VOL. II

"Ubi Charitas, ibi Deus"

LONDON
RICHARD BENTLEY AND SON
Publishers in Ordinary to Her Majesty the Queen
1877

[All Rights Reserved]

Bungay
CLAY AND TAYLOR, PRINTERS

CONTENTS OF VOL. II.

CHAPTER I.
1849.

Happiness of vocation—Reflections of the author—Natalie's Postulancy—Testimony of her companions—Her firmness—Her simplicity—Her humility—She commences her Noviciate—Letters to her Sisters 1

CHAPTER II.
1849.

End of Noviciate—Natalie is appointed Secretary at the Mother-house—Her aptitude for this position—Work—Prayer—Letter to her Sisters—Active and interior life of Natalie—The Mother-house and those who dwell there—Sisters in every part of the world—Correspondence of Natalie—Her close connection with the work of the Missionaries—A happy life—The author of these pages sees her for the first time in the Religious habit ... 26

CHAPTER III.
1850—1854.

Trials—Natalie returns to Montrouge—The Cholera at Paris—Devotedness of the Sisters—Their joy to die—

Natalie is attacked—She is in extreme danger—She recovers and returns to the Mother-house—Her conduct amidst her companions—Happiness of Natalie—Her unchanging affection for her relatives—Letters to her friend and to her Sisters—The Rev. Father Hermann—The War in the East—M. Anatole Demidoff 53

CHAPTER IV.

1855—1856.

Marie de Bombelles arrives at Versailles—Joy of the two friends at meeting again—Death of Count de Bombelles—Devotedness of his daughter—Her recovery after the death of her father—Her determination to enter the Religious life—Meeting and parting of Marie and Natalie—Last conversation at the Mother-house—Letters of Natalie to her Sisters—Death of Father de Ravignan—The Rev. Father Etienne—He takes Natalie to Rome—Audience with the Pope—Sister Natalie at the feet of Pius the Ninth—Departure for Florence—Interviews with M. Anatole Demidoff—Serious illness of Natalie—She is obliged to remain in Florence after the departure of Father Etienne—She returns to Paris—Death of Madame Swetchine 83

CHAPTER V.

1858.

Sister Natalie is appointed Superior of the Community of the Rue Saint Guillaume—Her repugnance to accept this post—Her submission—Her new duties and the qualities she evinced—Letters to her Sisters—Martyrdom of the companion of her childhood—Death of Viscount Des Cars—Death of Mademoiselle Françoise de Maistre—Acute sufferings of Natalie 127

CHAPTER VI.

1858.

Portrait of Sister Natalie at this period of her life—Her qualities as Superior—Her intercouse with her Sisters—With children—With her friends—With God—Letter from a young workwoman—Sister Natalie's affection for Russia—The gift she possessed for instructing and consoling—The Countess N——   156

CHAPTER VII.

1865.

Interior life of Sister Natalie—Visit of Father Hermann—Journey of Sister Natalie with the Rev. Father Etienne—She goes to Gratz—She there meets her Sisters again—Goes to Vienna and meets Marie de Bombelles—Returns to Paris—Cholera breaks out at St. Petersburg—She solicits from the Empress of Russia the favour of going there—Refusal—Community life—Sister Agnes   ... 190

CHAPTER VIII.

Community life—Its results—Sister Natalie's illness increases—Cholera in Paris—Letters—A Sister's Story—Increasing fervour of Sister Natalie—War in 1870—Siege—Courage and energy of Sister Natalie—Her devotion towards the Sacred Heart—Reflections—The Commune—Imminent danger—The Convent is surrounded by barricades—Conflagrations in the city—The Mother-house is saved—Fighting during the last days—The Sisters and the insurgents   221

CHAPTER IX.

1871—1874.

End of the struggle—Sister Natalie is sent to Dax—She returns to Paris—Her state becomes more alarming—Her end approaches—Saintliness of her last days—The Refectory—The Infirmary—Submission to the will of God—Her only disquiet—The kind supplies she receives from Countess N—— —Last moments—Her death—Letter from one of her companions—Her burial 259

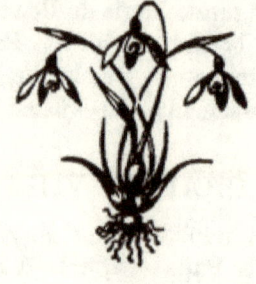

SISTER NATALIE NARISCHKIN.

CHAPTER I.
1849.

"AM happy!" How frequently had Natalie uttered these words since she had entered on her new life! We so seldom hear this exclamation in a world where happiness is nevertheless ardently and universally sighed for, and the faintest appearance of it hailed as a hope or a promise without which few would care to live, that that expression is worth attention. No doubt that the wicked, in the midst of their guilty pleasures, often give utterance to such a sentiment, and that in their moments of legitimate and innocent joy the good also feel and declare themselves happy. But even the purest and sweetest earthly bliss is so evanescent that it is hard to realize its existence before it vanishes; and when it has departed, life remains for some an anticipated hell; for others, a sad period of expectancy, only brightened by the rays of Divine hope. This is the fatal price which has too often to be paid for the temporary enjoyment of this world's happiness; and the more keen and exhilarating have been those short-lived joys, the more deep and bitter are the wounds they leave behind them when they disappear.

This is so evident that it amounts to a truism; and yet one cannot but revert to the thought, when those same words are uttered with a different and unearthly accent, which indicates that the happiness they express will be neither precarious nor transient—nay! that from its very nature it will go on increasing and enlarging, until the day when it will be merged in immortality, the mere foretaste of which triumphed over the trials and vicissitudes of time.

Yes, I will never cease to repeat it! I cannot understand that, at an epoch when the human mind is continually engaged in elaborating a thousand systems—the object of which is, after all, to afford happiness to the greatest possible number of persons—people close their eyes, shut their ears, and stifle their judgment, in order not to see those happy faces, not to hear those joyful voices, not to listen to those who would prove to them that what they are seeking others have found, and that the problem has been practically solved which they are vainly striving to fathom.

But we shall be asked, perhaps, if it is our wish to see the world emptied for the sake of filling the cloisters. This vain desire has indeed never entered our mind. But we look upon it as a general law, in accordance with the fate of humanity, to consider those souls whom God has called to an exceptional vocation, as beacon-lights set on a height to show us the way to true happiness. We shall not tread that path with the same swiftness, we shall not reach the summits they have reached, we shall not drink of the full cup of unearthly joy which is the portion of God's chosen ones on earth, but we may taste a drop of it perhaps, and attain to a higher insight into the promises He has made to us. Life will then no longer be shrouded in dark mystery. If we are amongst the happy few of this world, we shall learn to prize our joys at their right measure, and be prepared to resign what can only last a while; or, if we belong to that far more numerous crowd to whom blessings were once given, now for ever passed away,—or to those, perhaps, yet more to be pitied, who have never known any happiness,—we may aspire to a yet more exquisite joy. Those who meekly accept the burthen God lays upon them may share the blessed lot of those who have voluntarily assumed them.

"The world begins well," says an author I have already quoted,* "and ends badly. Nothing which has not the transforming touch of Divine grace can really please and

---

* "Public Life of our Lord Jesus Christ," Father Coleridge, S.J., vol. I., chap. xii., page 171.

hold the soul or the heart. On the other hand, God begins by what seems hard and stern, by commandments and rules, limitations on our liberty, and restraints upon our nature. 'The fear of the Lord is the beginning of wisdom,' and He first of all trains us to holy discipline. But He raises us higher and higher; He gives us new tastes and perceptions; and when we come to be able to enjoy spiritual delights, they are like the good wine which was kept to the last. At first the Cross is hard to bear, the doctrine of humility is difficult, it is a pain to conquer and subdue ourselves; but when once these things find the palate of the soul capable of tasting their sweetness, there is no longer any room left for any sweetness but theirs. And if it is so in this life, if the yoke and burthen of our Lord even here are easy and light to those who take them up courageously, much more is the parable underlying the miracle of Cana true in the next world, which is the last thing which our merciful God has in store for us—the last and the best."

* * * *

The day that Natalie crossed the threshold of the Hospital of Montrouge she gave herself up so completely to God that there was not any transition time, as it were, between her life in the world and in religion. Never for a moment was the hand which had been set to the plough, withdrawn; never was a glance cast backward. In the noviciate she acquired the habits of her new mode of existence, and learned the way to devote all the powers of her soul, mind, and body in a new direction; but from the first moment, her humility, simplicity, and obedience, were what they ever afterwards remained; and in the meek servant of the poor nothing recalled the young girl who had spent her early years in the midst of the most brilliant cosmopolite society of Europe.

Once, however, she and others were involuntarily reminded of her former position, and that was when a broom was for the first time put into her hands: the awkwardness with which she handled it dismayed her. Her companions could not help smiling at the novice's clumsiness, but were still more struck with her gentle patience, her assiduous efforts to do better, the pleasure with which she received reproofs, and her perfect good-temper and readiness to be instructed. One of them said, "There was a simple grace about her which won all hearts."

On the 24th of March, 1848, she left Montrouge, and began her noviciate in that house in the Rue de Bac she had so long known and loved. During that year of probation her correspondence was limited to a few letters to her sisters, the tone of which shows that she had not been deceived in her expectation that the noviciate would prove to her a foretaste of paradise. We find nothing changed in her tender love for her relatives, and her unaffected interest about them; but she seems to be writing from a world like to ours indeed as to prayer and labour, love and suffering—but full of that joy which arises from peace with God, with men, and with self.

This halt, as it were, of a year's duration, before the beginning of a life of incessant activity which does not leave unoccupied a single hour of the day, must have been very congenial to one who had so strong an attraction to meditation and silence. To live a while in this retirement, in a place shut out from earth and widely open on the side of heaven, realized Natalie's dearest dreams; and they were probably the only days of her life during which she was able fully to indulge the feelings which filled her soul. But though long hours are given to silence and prayer during the noviciate, the future Sister of Charity has also to exercise herself in the various duties she will have hereafter to perform. Natalie's zeal, obedience, exact attention, and quick comprehension of her new occupations never failed, and her natural sweetness, intelligence, and charm of manner, assisted her in their practice. The thought that she was working for God never left her for a single moment, or that of preparing her soul—by watchfulness, mortification, and the habitual surrender of her own will—for the greater enjoyment of the moments she was in His immediate presence, and could satisfy her yearning desires of love and union with Him. One of her companions who has favoured me with these details, says, with a simple depth of thought, " The greater is the heart the more needy it is, for nothing on earth can fill it. This is why our dear Sister Natalie never shrank from any sacrifice, in the hope of ever gaining a greater nearness to God." To say the truth, these sacrifices were so generously made that it astonished her to find that others thought anything of them, especially as, at the same time she was edifying her superiors and her companions, she herself lamented over her continued inability to fulfil properly the duties she had to perform in the house and the kitchen.

One of her directresses, touched by her

earnest efforts, gave her a private lesson in her room as to the manner of handling a broom, and also as to several other acquirements of that sort. Natalie took the greatest pains to profit by these instructions, but neither during her noviciate, nor her subsequent residence at the Mother-house, did she quite succeed in mastering these difficulties. Later on, however, she overcame them all; and by the time she was herself placed at the head of a community, was able to turn her hand to the most minute details of domestic work, as well as merely to govern its general administration. But at the time we are speaking of, the humble novice was far from foreseeing that the office of Superioress would ever be assigned to her, or desiring it. Her delight was to obey, for it was the only way of satisfying that spirit of humility produced by the love of God.

As to wearing a habit which was the badge of her devotion to that love, and to that of the poor, it was her joy and her pride. How could she have felt it a humiliation to serve those of whom our Lord has said, "What you do unto them you do unto me." We do not find many details as to acts which had no value in her eyes but that of obedience—to her the dearest of all virtues—in the brief sketch by which the Community of the Sisters of Charity commemorates the merits of a deceased Sister for the sole benefit of her companions. Those who drew it up were not likely to see anything remarkable in facts which make up the whole of their own lives. What we call charity, self-devotion, and heroism, they look upon as the simple fulfilment of daily duties. This is one of the difficulties of our present work, and the reason why those who might be supposed to feel most interest in it afford but little assistance to a biographer. To speak of one Sister of Charity is to describe them all. To praise her is to praise all her companions, and they detest praise of every sort. It is of all things in this world, next to sin, what they most loathe.

Time went by quickly. The year was drawing to an end, and to prove that we have not exaggerated Natalie's merits we may mention here that her companions called her "the flower of the seminary." But before we follow her in the new phase about to open in her life, it will be well to transcribe some letters she wrote during her noviciate. They were addressed to her two sisters, Elisabeth and Catherine, who were then together at Trieste, where the official duties of the Baron de Petz had fixed their residence. This change of abode, and family affairs connected with it, occupied Natalie in her retirement, for she never could remain indifferent to the welfare of her relatives:

"*Paris, May* 16*th*, 1848.

"My beloved Sisters,

"I waited a little to write till I could give you tidings of our dear Alexander. At last—the day before yesterday—I had the happiness of hearing from him. His letter was dated April 10th. As I felt sure, his silence proceeded only from want of leisure to write. I concluded that he had gone straight to Moscow, and wrote immediately to uncle Alexis to tell him of your letters, and to beg him to forward them immediately to Alexander, wherever he may be. I hope and I pray that God may have inspired you to write, long ago, directly to Moscow, for these delays and losses of time are injurious to your interests, and make me a little anxious. Not that I have not a great confidence as to the future, for I have very particularly committed you to the care of Divine Providence, and recommended to God all my wishes for you, whenever I have the happiness to be in His presence. But still I look forward impatiently to a letter from Trieste, which will tell me that my prayers have been heard. I have had a line from Edward *—written in great haste in the interval of his warlike avocations—in which he speaks of your silence, and laments it. Poor dear brother! He is so unhappy, and his affection for his dear Marie's rela-

---

* Her brother-in-law, M. de Valois.

tives so touching, that he deserves to be a little spoilt. I answered his letter at once, but who knows if, in the midst of all these commotions, mine will have reached him! Oh, my dear sisters, what a sad world it is! What disorder and confusion everywhere! More than ever it seems to me easy, and even necessary, to rise above it, and to detach ourselves from what is not really worthy of our cares. I feel ashamed when I think of so many years past and misspent, and I find consolation in the hope that God's infinite goodness will make that shame profitable to my soul and to His glory. Oh! do let us, my very dear ones, detach ourselves more and more from this world. Let us be like pilgrims, who care for absolutely nothing but the road they follow, and the end to which it leads!

"We have had a most beautiful month

of May! How my dear Kate would have enjoyed it!—and then, quite a shower of consoling graces. For instance, the other day, the Sister Infirmarian, in trying to lift a patient from her bed, staggered and fell. The sick Sister, falling also upon her, dislocated the neck of the Infirmarian so badly that the passage of the throat was almost obstructed. The surgeons tried some remedies which proved quite useless, and then declared there was no hope but in an operation which might prove very dangerous. For six days she remained in a state of indescribable suffering; her leg and arm became paralysed; and during all that time she could neither sleep, nor swallow anything but a few drops of liquid, and that with intense pain. Well, on Sunday the 7th of May, the Novena of the Translation of St. Vincent's relics began at St.

Lazare; the sufferer joined in it with all her companions, and applied to her neck a bit of St. Vincent's habit. Her faith increased, and also her pains. On the Thursday she entreated to be carried to the Shrine, and difficult as it was to do this, it was thought right to comply with her request. From that moment she felt certain of her cure. On the Tuesday, with a great deal of trouble, she was placed on a stretcher, and at four o'clock in the morning carried to St. Lazare. A Mass was said, and as it was going on she felt strange sensations in her bones. Her arm and leg recovered the power of motion; her head its position; and then after receiving Holy Communion, she felt so well that, without any assistance, she left the stretcher, knelt down with perfect ease, and walked home. Since that moment she has been in better health than ever. You may imagine, my dear ones, the effect produced amongst us by this miraculous event—the joy, the gratitude, the deep feeling it produced! We could not help seeing in it a fresh proof of the special goodness of our Lord to this dear house.

"As I cannot write to my friends, will one of you, dear sisters, communicate this fact to Marie de Bombelles, Mrs. Neville, and Thérèse (de Thurn). I know all the interest and the pleasure they will feel in it, and Miana also; and to think that, notwithstanding all my wretchedness and unworthiness, I am in the midst of all this—I know they will thank God for it.

"I want, too, my dear Marie de Bombelles to know that, on the day before I entered the noviciate, I wrote her a long letter, in which I enclosed one to Father

Ferrari. Probably in the midst of all the agitations of that moment in Italy, these letters were lost. Tell her how affectionately I kiss her, and that I always pray for her and all of them. I am so glad to think of Catherine being with you, especially since you have told me the happiness it is to you. Still, my dear friends, your last letters made me sad. I should so like to know all your affairs arranged. Try soon to write to me something pleasant about that. I think often of the Grand Duchess Olga, since Edward wrote to me that she interests herself about you. And then, as to other consolations, they all come from God.

"Farewell, with many tender kisses.

"Your affectionate sister,

"NATALIE."

"*Paris, November* 19*th,* 1848.

"Dear darling sisters, my good little Elisabeth,—what have you thought of my silence, which has lasted some days longer than usual, and that when you had so prettily asked me to wish you joy? Oh, yes, you may be sure that from my heart I wish you joy, and rejoice in your happiness with all the depth and extent of my affection for you. But I thought it would be better to make this sacrifice, and even to let you long a little for my letter, than to ask for a dispensation from the rule, which would have been, no doubt, charitably granted to me. I therefore refrained from doing so. To-day, when there is no impediment, I cannot but feel that the pleasure it gives me to write to you is twice as great. Dear little sister—or rather my dear sisters—and you also, my dear

Tonnino, whom you know well I never separate from you in my heart,—so you are all again full of joy and hope. Keep up, dearest Elisabeth, that happy trust you now feel, and which will always support you through all the trials of life. Do not let the thought of A—— make you anxious. It is not with you as it was with her,—the case of a first child. Be full of confidence in the protection of the Blessed Virgin during that beautiful month of May consecrated to her, and that seems to promise you a happiness for which I promise you to pray and to get prayers.

"Good Sister Barba has been so busy that she never could find time to write to you. She will make amends for this omission; and in the mean time both she and our good Father Aladel, who wishes you every happiness, are earnestly praying for your intention. Oh, my dear ones, I am so happy in God's house! Nothing can equal this happiness, which literally increases every day. Thank and bless our Lord for me. I have so little myself to give Him—this wretched heart of mine, —nothing else. Well, if only it can be occupied throughout eternity in praising Him, I ask nothing more.

"Bénédicte de Maistre is married, and lives at Bergamo; but her husband was very ill at the time that Count Rodolph de Maistre paid me a visit, and he was very anxious about him. All that charming little society of the governor's palace at Nice is now dispersed. They have left that brilliant post, and are living in retirement near Turin. The Count had brought to Paris one of his sons, who means, I think, to become a son of the great Ignatius.

How many events, how many changes everywhere! Nothing on earth will ever be lasting—nothing but what religion holds out and gives. Happy those who find in it guidance and help. Take great care of yourself, dear little Elisabeth, and try always—you and Kate—to love God and the Blessed Virgin more and more. Oh, you will also be happy one day!—I feel sure of it. Farewell; God bless you all.

"Your affectionate Sister,

"NATALIE."

CHAPTER II.

1849.

IT was on the 13th of January, 1849, that Natalie was clothed in the habit of the Sisters of St. Vincent of Paul. This great and important moment of her life had been hastened in her case, and the time of her probation shortened by two months, in consequence of the great proofs of virtue she had given during her noviciate. We cannot know exactly, but we are inclined to think that if a choice had then been allowed to one who wanted only to obey, the new daughter of St. Vincent of Paul would have liked to be employed in the works most specially belonging to the Order she had entered. But instead of that, and though they had ascertained that her courage and devotedness would have been equal to all the duties, the sights, and the perils which Sisters of Charity must accept and brave, her Superiors took the unexpected resolution of setting her to a quite different sort of work. All Natalie's companions possessed, like her, the above-mentioned qualities, but she was endowed with gifts not easily to be met with.

Her facility in letter-writing can be judged of by the specimens we have given of her correspondence. She spoke and wrote French like a native of France, and had not forgotten the language of her own country. English, German, and Italian she also spoke and wrote with fluency, and had a clear, neat, and pleasing manner of expressing her thoughts. The post now assigned to her was that of Secretary, at the central house of the Rue de Bac, at Paris, and her work, a constant correspondence with the houses of the Order in every part of the world.

Thus she remained, for many years after her noviciate, in that dearly-loved house, engaged in important and interesting avocations, which it would not have occurred to her beforehand to covet, but in the accomplishment of which she found so much happiness, that obedience seemed to have regulated her life during that time in the most perfect accordance with her tastes and her natural aptitude, as well as with her twofold spiritual attractions. On the one hand, she was not severed from the poor—they always enter into part of the life of a Sister of Charity; but on the other hand, the duties she had to perform allowed her to divide the greatest portion of her time between work, recollection, and prayer; and thus to satisfy that love of contemplation which equalled the ardour of her active charity. So intensely did she enjoy this phase of her religious life, that it was only when she was compelled to accept other employment that she knew the cost of the effort obedience exacts. But this was not to happen till long afterwards, and we find her writing letters to her dearest friends, which enable us to judge of her feelings during those first years of her religious life:

"*Paris, March 4th*, 1849.

"It has arrived at last—that day on which I can write—my dearest, to tell you the great news. There has been a little delay in communicating it to you, but you will not be the less glad to hear of it. About two months ago I was clothed in our holy habit. Our Lord gave it to me, as a New Year's gift, on the Russian New Year's Day—the 13th of January; and how many other blessed gifts does not that one gift allow me to hope! When I think that on such a day, only five years ago, I was satisfied with the merest frivolities, and that now nothing can assuage the thirst of that same heart of mine but Jesus Christ and His adorable cross! Oh yes, my little Sache, I am at the height of my wishes!—and although in the service of this dear Master every office is alike, and every place the same—whether in exile, or poverty, or repose, or activity—I do look upon it as a special blessing that I remain in this dear house, which is so holy a home, and where we feel as if God's graces were showered upon us.

"What can I say in answer to your letters, and about the joy they give me, but that you are always my dearly-loved little sister, whom I associate every day, and with all my heart, in the good works I am engaged in? Tell Teresina Massa,* that I thank her and her good brothers for their remembrance of me before God. I feel so much interested in all you tell me about them. Tell her also to ask those two good Fathers,† Gaetano and Luigi, to pray for Catherine and Elisabeth, who

---

* She and her brothers were those youthful friends of Natalie, who at Sorrento, in 1835, endeavoured in their childlike way to convert her.

† Father René Massa died a martyr in China. Four of his brothers had also devoted themselves to the foreign missions.

are acquainted with them. I think the Baronne de Massa must be very happy to see all her children called to so high a privilege; such graces cannot be sufficiently appreciated. Marie de Raigecourt also entered the Order of the Visitation a few days after I arrived at Paris last year. Poor Albertine de la Ferronnays is staying here now with her brother Charles. She is pious, courageous, and resigned,* but very sad as you may well fancy. Do, dear little friend, tell Monseigneur Mislin that I have leave to accept the precious relic he offers to send me, and that I shall be most grateful for that present. Would you also add to your letter that I was very much touched by his recollection of me at the sepulchre of our Lord, and that I look upon it as a special grace to have been

---

* She had just lost her mother.

associated with the fervent souls for whom he was praying there?

"Marie de Bombelles gives me some hopes that Providence may sooner or later bring us together again. But how can we reckon upon anything in this world? What is there certain except eternity?—the only thought on which we can securely repose. Oh, let us strive hard to ensure its being a happy one!

"What becomes of my poor M——? I often sigh when I think of her; but there is nothing we may not hope from that Divine blood, shed for us—that is my only faith, my only hope—for sinners, for the whole world, and myself. Thanks also for Miss McCarthy's kind remembrances. I am much interested and pleased by all you tell me about her. If you can find out where Father Ferrari is, do manage to give him tidings of me, and commend me both to him and to Father Curci. I look upon them as my first Fathers, and I promised Father Ferrari never to forget that I am his daughter. I shall keep my promise! Oh! when will the happy time arrive when religion will triumph and reign in every heart?

"Well, my dear little friend, I am obliged to leave off. I leave you in the Immaculate Heart of our dear Mother. Pray to her for me. I will write a line to Sachinka de Serra-Capriola, but give my love to my other friends, and beg them to excuse me, as now I cannot possibly keep up a large correspondence. Many kind messages to the Marchesa Gargallo.

"Your affectionate Sister,

"NATALIE."

TO THE SAME.

"*Paris, May* 4*th*, 1849."

"One single line in haste, my dear little friend, to thank you for your kind letter and its contents. A souvenir from Gaeta,* and another that speaks of nothing but the purest love of God! How precious all this is! Do pray that that love may never diminish in my heart. If we persevere in this petition we may hope indeed that this holy fire will never go out. But that is not enough,—I want it never to diminish! Oh! it is too great a happiness to belong to a Master as good as Him I serve. To feel oneself a poor little worm in His sight, and yet to know one belongs to Him!—this is indeed happiness; that thought, whenever it occurs to one, seems to fill my heart with joy. You can

---

* The Holy Father was there at that time.

never bless God enough for me! I was so glad to meet again the excellent Abbé Gerbet; and some days ago I had the happiness of being called to the parlour to see good Father Curci. I need not tell you, dear friend, that we talked about you, and then about our blessed, our Divine Lord. Those sort of conversations do one so much good. I should like to describe to you all the overflowing gratitude which fills my soul, but it is better, perhaps, silently to dwell on such thoughts; and then I am much pressed for time, and I have said enough to induce you to thank God for me.

"Pray much for my dear little Elisabeth, who by this time must, I suppose, be a mother."

Three months afterwards, she wrote to the same friend, at Naples:

"*Paris, August 3rd*, 1849.

" A tiny word only, to say that I have ventured to send you a little parcel for Trieste, and that I forward another, by the hands of our good M. Spaccapietra, for the same place, hoping that you will be able to send it more directly than I could do here, through the Embassy. They are both for my dear Catherine. Thank God, the accounts from Trieste are good as to health, and as to the dear little Marie Valentine. Dear Tonnino's absence mixes indeed a little sorrow with Elisabeth's joy, but she bears it with tolerable resignation. She feels that having received so much she must also give something in return, and that there is no unmixed happiness in this world. Anyhow, I do long for the end of this sad war, and I continually pray and offer up the precious and Divine

Blood of our Lord Jesus Christ for that intention. But the designs of Providence are as wise as they are impenetrable. We must adore them in silence, till it pleases God to send a ray of light on the whole surface of the political world.

"I send you to-day only a small simple picture, always begging you to pray for your little Sister of Charity. Oh! if you knew how much God asks from those to whom He gives much! But if you only knew, also, how sweet it is to give Him everything we can, at every hour, at every moment, without an instant's relaxation! Ask that I may have an unalterable fidelity and generosity; even in the smallest things I never forget you. If you should see our dear Sisters Vinsonneau and Messine on their way, one to the new foundation at Averse, the other to

Giovinazzo, they will tell you more about me than I have time myself to do—if indeed they can throw away any of theirs for that purpose. My love to all my friends. I write to no one. My affectionate respects to your parents."

From this time forward her letters to her relatives and acquaintances become more rare; she could not find leisure for correspondence, even within the authorized limits. Her heart was ever faithful to her friends, but the key-note, so to speak, of her spirit is more clearly marked as time advances.

In the beginning of 1850, she writes: " One more word to-day, to thank you for your little letter, and to beg for the continuance of your fervent recollection of me at the feet of our Lord. The happiness He lets me enjoy in His service is such that I cannot even attempt to speak of it. When the remembrance of the past rises up before me, the weight of gratitude I feel is quite overwhelming.

"You understand me, my dear little sister, but you never will know what He alone can know, what He alone can discern, as to the nature of those feelings. Oh! for my part I may well exclaim, 'Let my tongue cleave to the roof of my mouth, if I can ever forget what I owe to the Lord!'

"Our good Sister Gottofrey has asked me what she was to say to you from me. The messages I sent were but the repetition of what I write, and can never repeat often enough. She told me of all the good you and your parents are doing. You can fancy what a sweet response her words found in the heart of your little sister. We did not see much of each other—Sœur Gottofrey and I—because, what with the retreats, and then all the work and the business of our Ark, it is almost impossible to converse. But it did not signify, a few minutes were enough to make me love that dear Sister. This is soon done, when two persons have the happiness of being enrolled under the same standard. It seems as if there was a sacred watchword for minds and for hearts which unites everything in a common centre. It is then a happiness to meet. No sooner do we know than we love one another; we feel that we are all the children of the same father, the spouses of the same crucified Lord, possessing the same hopes and aspiring to the same happiness, which is nothing but the sovereign good—Heaven our portion, and our inheritance for eternity.

"Farewell, in the expectation of the

happy day which will unite us all. Excuse this scrawl, and do not forget that what I ask of you is thanksgiving,—never can you offer up too much of it for your unworthy little sister,

"NATALIE."

"P.S. My respects to your good parents. Say a thousand things for me to Sachinka, to Hélène Suchtelen, and both their families. I cannot write to them now, my time is not my own—tell them so. A happy slavery, I assure you; my only regret is not to have known it sooner."

These affectionate letters, so full of love of God and of her friends, were scribbled by Natalie during the few minutes of leisure snatched from the beloved occupations of her daily life. She had a right to say that her time was not her own, for she had made an offering of it, as well as of herself, in the most unrestricted manner. But besides all that satisfied and nourished her soul in her vocation, it must be admitted that she was employed at that moment in a most interesting and attractive occupation.

What are, after all, the questions which absorb in the world the minds of those who are not given up to mere frivolity, and who know how to fill up their lives with interests worthy of the name? Do they not all relate in some way or other to the national or international questions which concern the improvement of the human race, and the greatest possible diminution of the evils inherent to it? And amongst those evils, do they not principally reckon the sufferings, the misery, and the ignorance which affect, everywhere, the majority of men? And if, to soften the first, to relieve the second, and to dissipate the third, is to perform what—in the language of Christians—are called works of mercy, does not the world call them, in its own phraseology, works of civilization? We may well ask, then, what is the exclusive work of the Sisters of Charity, but to relieve the sick, to help the poor, and to instruct the ignorant. Such are also the objects of the zealous and eminent persons above alluded to; but it must be admitted that, generally speaking, they speak and discuss, and compare and write, more than they act. And if some of them do set on foot, at home, some undertaking more or less successful, it is seldom that we see them leave their homes to carry the results of their experience to the furthest ends of the world; whereas the daily acts which the Sisters are constantly performing under our eyes they likewise accomplish in every part of the universe—that Divine charity which summons and sends them to the help of the poor, extends from one pole to the other, and from the furthest East to the remotest West. Their white cornette is a symbol of hope and consolation for the most destitute, the most suffering, the most miserable of men. Nor is their devotion an isolated one. What they do is not the result of zeal in a few heroic souls, such as are everywhere to be found—to the praise of humanity. They form one closely-united family, animated by the same spirit. In number and in discipline they also make up an army of women, of whom it can be said, that " No dangers fright them and no labours tire "— who willingly accept interminable banishments from their native land, and too often a speedy, sometimes a bloody death. Then as soon as the fatal effects of pestilential climates or the hands of cruel men have thinned their ranks, the Mother-house is appealed to—that house so justly called an ark by Sister Natalie, for it seems indeed to float as a sacred refuge on the stormy sea of Parisian life—and then immediately a fresh supply are joyfully told off to supply the vacant places, and none complain but those left behind.

One day, in 1854, I happened to be present when a young Sister arrived from a house at some distance with a commission from her Superior to the Mother-General, who seemed delighted when she appeared, and said, " that instead of returning to the place she came from, she would have to start immediately for one of the ambulances in the Crimea, where cholera and fatigue had made great havoc amongst the Sisters." The young Sister's only answer was an inquiry whether as she had not brought her apron with her she could go and fetch it. "No, there would not be time for that," was the reply; "what she wanted would be given to her." No other explanation was necessary, and the young Sister quietly and simply departed for her distant and perilous post.

If we admire, and with reason, military discipline, is it not still more striking to witness voluntary self-devotion accomplishing acts of such manly courage? And shall we not endeavour to discover the principle which enables women, with their weak natures, to accomplish what a feeling of honour cannot always secure in men and soldiers without the additional safeguards afforded by the fear of public disgrace and of severe punishment?

Be that as it may: it may be easily

conceived that to be mixed up with the sort of universal action, and to follow in all its details the works of this great kingdom of charity, must be a most absorbing and interesting occupation, and that it gives the soul and heart a higher sustenance than that which satisfies women of the world, even when they are not particularly frivolous.

Such was Natalie's life for ten successive years. All her remarkable intellectual gifts were thus devoted to the highest and most useful labour, and this labour was the occasion of her exercising faculties she had never, till then, been conscious of possessing. She acquired the strictest habits of order, a quickness of decision, and aptitude in the transaction of business, which as time went on quite astonished those who had been chiefly struck by her simplicity and humility. These virtues were always conspicuous in Sister Narischkin, even when living amongst those who were all humble and simple.

But the importance of this assiduous work, and the very interest of a correspondence which sometimes brought, on the same day, letters from Rome, Constantinople, China, Greece, England, Germany, the United States, would have been injurious to health, if its hours had not been regularly and judiciously distributed. Time was so arranged as to afford needful rest, and measured so as not to affect health; a useful variety was secured in the occupations of each day. For so fervent a soul the sweetest repose consisted in the hours spent in the chapel she had so much and so long loved, where she had so earnestly prayed in former days, and so ardently asked that Blessed One, whose holy presence had sanctified this sanctuary, to obtain for her graces which had now been realized beyond her hopes. What her soul reaped during those long hours of prayer, of meditation, and holy instructions, could not be ascertained in detail; but it was guessed at by those who beheld her ever-increasing serenity, and her constant efforts to accomplish, with the greatest possible perfection, every one of her actions. Sometimes, also, it could be discerned by the radiant and beaming expression of her countenance.

It was towards the end of the year of her noviciate that I saw her again for the first time since our abrupt and sad parting in 1843. I was staying then, for a few days only, in Paris; and hastening to the house in the Rue de Bac, I asked to see her. I was told that an instruction was being given at that moment in the chapel, and that as soon as it was finished she would be informed of my wish to see her.

I accordingly waited, and waited a long time, occupied meanwhile with the reflections always suggested by that house in which poverty, simplicity, and austerity are accompanied by such a prevailing peacefulness. Looking at the walls, I read the inscriptions upon them, amongst others this one: "It is worth while to live without pleasure in order to die without regret;" and again—"A God to serve, a soul to save, a Heaven to win"—and many others besides. I thought of Natalie as I had left her; I could not picture her to myself as I was about to see her.

At last she came in and quietly advanced towards me. When she kissed me with all the affectionate warmth of other days; when under her cornette I beheld again that same countenance, that same smile, of which I had preserved so vivid a remembrance; I felt a great emotion and a great joy, and at the same time a sort of astonishment. Far from being changed in appearance, or looking less well than before, her usually pale face was flushed with the brightest colour. This struck me so much that I could not help remarking it. "Oh! it will go off," she said; "I am not always so—the fact is," she added, "that I have been spending an hour by the fire." What she meant was, that she had been hearing about God, and spending some time in His presence!

The remembrance of these words, which seemed to escape from her heart, has many a time warmed my own.

CHAPTER III.

1850—1854.

ALTHOUGH happiness is undoubtedly one of the mysterious fruits of a life of sacrifice, it would be erroneous to suppose that to secure it is the object of those who embrace that life in its most perfect form. It is granted to them in super-addition to what they have sought in it, but vocation is in reality the voluntary acceptance of the cross — the spontaneous choice of the way which Jesus Christ has trod, and where He calls His dearest friends to follow Him. It is not, therefore, in the least our object to draw for our readers a fanciful picture of the religious life, full of natural gratifications as well as supernatural joys. Such a strange idea would be in opposition to the invariable conditions of all that is great upon earth. Everything worthy of being esteemed undergoes more or less in this world the inevitable law of suffering, and it is in proportion to the efforts they have cost that we measure their value. How could it be otherwise with sanctity, the highest and most sublime of all states? The human heart, whatever is its destiny, suffers and enjoys with equal intensity. But suffering belongs to this world, whereas enjoyment will attain its perfection in the next.

It is not therefore happiness *instead* of suffering that so many fervent and generous hearts come to look for in the shade of the sanctuary. It is happiness *in* suffering. First, in that suffering which nature must always experience in trampling over itself, in order perfectly to imitate Christ; and then, in trials of a still higher kind, which they alone are acquainted with,—for it is only in the path of perfection that they are found. It is not for us to speak to those chosen souls of what may be called their own Divine trials. We can only guess at their nature by what saints have written and expressed. But we can explain to others, that just as the sun when it rises in the sky reveals to sight a variety and an extent of prospects in the natural world which in the dim light of dawn had been indiscernible, so does the Divine light, as it grows more intense, exhibit to a soul heights and depths and wonderful developments of perfection which sometimes dazzle and overpower it. Longing to penetrate into these hitherto unknown regions, it would fain advance, scale those heights, and plunge into those abysses; and then the humility of such a soul gives utterance to strange accents, which we who witness its virtues can hardly understand, and can scarcely conceive to be sincere. It is not a judgment they form, as much as a comparison, between their own spiritual state, not as compared with that of other imperfect creatures more sinful than themselves, but with an ineffable image which reveals itself more and more to their mental vision. They do not count the steps by which they have drawn near to it, but only those they have to make in order to reach it; and this union of perception of desire and of conscious weakness produces a special suffering, sometimes more trying and difficult to endure than physical pain. Its last and highest degree consists in the feeling of being unworthy of the happiness so ardently sought, and in the fear of not answering to the love which holds out that bliss.

These are things, of course, not generally felt or understood. They are, no doubt, imparted according to the graces already received, or in store for particular souls; but they are real and true, and, after all, not strange, if we call to mind that, even as regards human affections, earthly love is attended by sufferings unknown to those who have never loved. It is the same with the purest, the most ardent, the most sublime of all affections. The all but inspired writer of the "Imitation of Christ," in speaking of Divine love, tells us, "No one can live and love without suffering."

Natalie was not exempted from this crucifying and strengthening trial, and it is remarkable that she went through that ordeal precisely during that happy period when more than at any other time her mode of life in religion was most in accordance with her natural tastes. But never for a single moment were her serenity or courage affected by those inward trials. They only served to increase her humility and that perfect love which lives on pure faith, and in the midst of darkness patiently waits for the infallible return of light. In spite, however, of her courage, and the perfect manner in which she continued to accomplish all the acts of her exterior life, it became evident that her health was beginning to suffer, and for some time it was found necessary to relieve her from the exact observance of her rule. In accordance with medical advice she was sent back for a while to Montrouge. Food more adapted to the delicate state of her health was provided, and so much care taken of her that she was soon well enough to return to the Mother-house. But before she arrived there, the cholera had attacked that dear home of hers. In the course of a few days three hundred sisters were taken ill with that fearful malady, and fifty of them died.

All who witnessed the aspect of the house, and the conduct of the sisters under these afflicting circumstances, were astonished and edified. Those who were seized with the terrible disease had but one single thought, not that of escaping death, but only of not dying in vain. Without fear and without regret they offered up their lives, some of them for their dear absent friends, some for a Sister in Religion—many in behalf of the whole community. This ardour for self-sacrifice went so far that the Superiors were actually obliged to put a stop to it, and to remind those who held their own lives so cheap that they had given them to our Lord Jesus Christ for the service of the poor, and that they were instructed "not to ask to die, but to live in order to work." This exhortation did not reach Natalie before she, too, in all the ardour of her zeal, had made that same offering, and it seemed as if it had been accepted. Coming out of the chapel one day, she was seized with such violent symptoms of the epidemic that her case was considered hopeless. Dear as all her children were to the excellent Superior, this daughter of hers was more than commonly precious. Natalie saw her look of consternation, and exclaimed, "Oh! don't be afraid! I think our Lord has granted my prayer. . . . I asked Him to let me die instead of some other Sister more useful than myself to our dear community. God is very good! and I am so happy to die."

One of the Sisters of the Mother-house, who never left her whilst she was ill, bears witness that a greater calm serenity and supernatural joy in the midst of such terrible pain had never been seen. Not one regret, not one earthly desire, crossed that soul which seemed already in heaven. She patiently awaited the coming of her Divine Spouse, in peaceful union with His good pleasure.

The venerable director, Father Aladel, who had been at once sent for, thought that the hour had indeed arrived for that angelic soul to take its flight to Heaven, but God preserved her for further labours. She recovered, and so completely was her health restored that she was soon able to resume her duties as Secretary, and to follow in every respect the rule of her Order without intermission and without fatigue.

Her companions saw her again at work amongst them, and watched as before the details of her holy life. One of them writes: "To meet her in the passages, to hear her speak, to have oneself a few words of conversation with her, was a joy to each one of us all." And yet, with the wonderful charm of her sweetness and gentleness, and when she was only a simple Sister, she showed that firmness of character which made her, when the time came, govern so well.

One day that she was sent with a message from the Superior she found several young Sisters who were talking loud and laughing at a time when the rule prescribes silence. One of them said, that when Sister Natalie came into the room, she seemed like an angelic apparition, and that her subdued and religious expression of countenance was enough without the utterance of a word to make them feel ashamed of the irregularity of their behaviour.

Natalie accepted with a smile the apologies of the Sister who relates this little incident, and said with that charitable simplicity which made her firmness so gentle, " O, dear sister, do not disturb yourself. I am sure some unforeseen circumstance amused you, and I know that it is then very difficult to help laughing." And as her companion was expressing her fears that she had given scandal, Natalie rejoined, "Oh no, I know you too well to be disedified. You have a heart disposed to sympathize with every one; I am sure that your merriment was an act of charity, not a proof of levity."

This young Sister, whose only defect was to be sometimes led by her affection for her companions and the pleasure of talking to them into slight infractions of the rule, never forgot Natalie's charitable observations. Her tender respect for her increased in consequence. "I admired" (these were her words) "the way in which she always saw the best side of things, and the charity which made her turn to a good purpose all she witnessed and heard. . . . She knew better than anybody how to appreciate what was right, and when truth allowed of it to excuse what was wrong. Oh, dear sister Narischkin, what holy recollections, what sweet and blessed reminiscences, you have left in our hearts!"

Natalie's rapid spiritual progress, her detachment from everything earthly, and total forgetfulness of self, did not make her less simple, less affectionate, less kind in her intercourse with her relatives and friends. Her nature was transfigured, if we may so speak, but in no ways changed. The following letters will add a few touches to the description we have given of her life at that time, and relate to the occurrences of those two years:

"*April* 14*th*, 1852.

"If everybody understood the secret of happiness contained in the acquiescence of the will, I am sure we should oftener meet with persons like that good Jesuit Father at Venice whom we had nicknamed the 'Father without crosses,' because he would never let it be said that God sent him any. 'What is a cross?' he used to say, making one with his fingers. 'Well, it is easy to undo it,' he would add, hastening to change their position. I have never forgotten this simple little illustration, which shows so clearly what we have to practise. For my part, my crosses are made only of straw, but even those will not be useless for eternity if they are borne in a right spirit."

TO THE VICOMTESSE DES CARS.

"*April* 19*th*, 1854.

"I cannot attempt to express how much I have felt and shared your grief.* All

---

* Count Lebzeltern, father of the Vicomtesse Des Cars, had just died at Naples.

the details you give me as to the death of
your dear father have affected me very
much. How happy are those souls, dear
friend, who leave this earth after securing
heaven by their resignation! Their departure makes us think more of our own,
and the thought of their bliss re-awakens
all our holy desires. Let these short
separations detach us more and more from
earth, and bring us nearer to heaven.
These feelings are so familiar to you that
I am not afraid of speaking to you in this
sense. . . . My poor Kate* has been on the
rack. It will be a happiness to her if she
can be near you. Alas! I often say to
myself—' Oh, why am I so happy in this
world, whilst those who are so dear to me
go through so many successive afflictions?

---

* Catherine Narischkin had at last resolved to become a Catholic.

This thought would break my heart if I gave way to it; I must leave everything to Him who sends trials, which are really favours and graces."

TO CATHERINE.

"*June 1st.*

"My letters were sent on the 30th, just before I received from Geneva the telegram containing the heart-rending news * so sad to both of us. Oh, poor Alexander! If the thought of God's boundless mercies did not fill me with hope, I do not know how I should find strength to bear such a blow—... and yet I am His; I adore His will, and love it above all things. But even one anxious thought about a soul, and especially so dearly loved a soul, has in it such poignant bitterness, that if I did not throw myself into the arms of God with

---

* The death of her brother.

entire abandonment, I could not endure it. Oh! my dear friends, for God's sake, who is so good, but likewise so just, think well on that one important subject—eternal salvation! . . . I have been treated on this occasion with the most tender compassion. My sisters are all wonderfully good to me. I have written to my good uncle Alexis, that as I was the first person of the family who had received notice of this event, I thought it a duty to communicate it to him.

"More than ever, my dear friends, I give you all to our Lord, that He may bind you all to Himself, and be your all in all in this world."

TO CATHERINE.

"*August 9th*, 1854.

"My dear good Sister,

"I am so glad to hear that you mean to make a pilgrimage with N——

before coming here. That idea rejoices me very much. Do it with a strong spirit of faith, dear Kate, and you will feel the benefit of it.

"The Des Cars are at last arrived. Sache was to write to you before going into the country, and I hope she will return to Paris at the time you will be here. Her visit was a great pleasure to me. She is so pious, so sensible, so edifying, and so very charitable!—and she understands the poor so well. Our Sisters at Naples had already told me all that she does for them, but I have had the happiness now of judging of it for myself.

"I was anxious to hear of you after all the earthquakes that have taken place on the whole line of the Pyrenees.*

---

* Her sister was then at Bagnères de Luchon.

Divine chastisements are afflicting on every side our poor France. Here, like almost everywhere else, the cholera is raging.* You would be astonished to see our Sisters rush to the assistance of the victims. Every day they are sent for, to go to villages almost abandoned, without help of any sort. Alas! my turn has not come; I suppose that Almighty God does not think me worthy of so great a favour; and yet I assure you that I would gladly give up even your visit in order to be sent to the sick. If you hear that this favour has been granted to me, thank our good God, my dear sister. What a joy it would be to die in that way, like a soldier on the field of battle!—for our warfare is the

---

* There is no allusion in her letters to the first invasion of the cholera, during which she was herself seized with the disease.

exercise of charity, and our battle-field the cottages of the poor.

"Dear Kate, I understand so well all you feel, and on that account I long for you to be in possession of the graces and helps you are in need of. Our good God assists us under such circumstances. I experienced it at Moscow, when in the midst of our relatives I had to keep my secret for eight months. I should like to send you the narrative of the conversion of Father Jean Marie Augustin Hermann, a discalced Carmelite. It is impossible to read anything more interesting. I have seen him in our chapel, where he said Mass; and hymns were sung to the Blessed Sacrament, the music of which he has composed. They are most beautiful. He was a Jew, and the intimate friend of Listz,—his life as worldly as could be. He used to laugh at everything religious, and now, by the sudden virtue and power of the Divine Eucharist, he has been in a moment transformed into a Saint—a St. John of the Cross! Alexander read the account of that conversion, and it edified him very much. Alas! when I remember that I had him here last year, that he came to our procession of Corpus Christi, and that I cannot look forward now to the blessed effects of those days of grace, my heart sinks within me; and, like you, dear Kate, I would give everything, and my life itself, if God would accept it, to recall him to life! But the vanity of this wish must only lead us to renew our sacrifice with the submission which God, who has required it, expects from us.

"I have just received a little line from Elisabeth, who is impatiently looking forward to your arrival. Poor dear sister, her happiness when Tonnino can be with her is dearly bought by the grief of his long absences. But she has so much faith, and is so grateful for the blessings God grants to her, that I feel hopeful as to her future. I assure you that I cannot keep her out of my thoughts. Oh, with what joy I shall welcome all the details you will give me about her! Come soon, dear sister!"

TO A FRIEND.

"I have long delayed thanking you for the double offering you sent me before your departure. The sum destined for the foreign missions will serve for the purchase of a chalice for the chapel of the new establishment at Damascus, which occupies us at this moment. I think the Sisters will start next month.

"I have sent a copy of the 'Life of Father Hermann' to Kate. As I happen to have another I will send it to you. I am sure that you will read it with interest. One feels inclined to exclaim with that chosen soul, 'Let us love Jesus, all the rest is nothing.' Yes, dear Sache, let us love Him, and may He ever be our all in all in this world."

"*December* 11*th*, 1854.

"The news from the East continues to bring us terrible details about our poor soldiers. With what veneration we ought to look on the military profession, when we think of the self-devotion of those who belong to it, and the sufferings they endure with such wonderful resignation, esteeming it a simple duty to accept death!

"The number who are sent to Constantinople invalided is daily increasing, and the sick and wounded arrive there in a state which it is heart-breaking to witness. Everything possible is done to alleviate their sufferings. Our good God inspires some compassionate souls with a charity which invents all sorts of methods of relief. It is to be hoped that the actual cessation of hostilities may last beyond the spring. What terrible bloodshed there has been under the walls of Sebastopol! I will tell you many details about it too long to write.

"The services yesterday in all the churches of Paris were wonderfully solemn. The glorious privilege of our Mother was openly and joyfully proclaimed."

TO HER SISTER.

"My Dear Kate,

"I cannot account for your silence, which grieves me very much, and I write to entreat you to let me hear from you. I don't know where and with whom you are; wherever you are, you certainly cannot be alone—there must be somebody who can tell me what you are doing.

"To-day is the Feast of your glorious patron Saint—St. Catherine. This makes me think of you still more than usual, and long to know how you are spending it. I must tell you, dear sister, and that with the hope of giving you scruples, that this silence of yours is the cause of many distractions in my prayers and spiritual duties; and though I do not wish you to bear the punishment, I should like to make you feel a little repentance. . . .

"How is my little Valentine? Was she very glad to see her aunt, with her hands full of presents? I form to myself many a picture of happy moments since your return to that family home, if indeed you are there, dear Kate; for where are you?—there is the question. I hear that Bébé Strozzi will soon be here. Please God, he will tell me something about you."

"P.S. Our Sister Marchand has been in Paris, and spoke to me of your visit. She said you had been so good and charming that they were all full of it. I hope this is always the case, and that you are so to all those around you."

TO HER FRIEND.

"I have just received your letter, dear little friend, and at the same time a bottle of the water of Jordan, sealed, and therefore genuine. My first thought was that it had arrived just in time for the baptism of the baby you are expecting, and I am sending it to the Rue de Grenelle, to be forwarded to you. We have in similar circumstances made presents of this water, which we often receive, and with the sanction of the Bishops it has been used, mixed with that of the baptismal fonts.

"If I am not mistaken, little Valentine Petz was baptized with water from the Jordan, which her father had brought back with him from his travels. For my part, I like to attach to it a peculiar virtue.

"I need not say that we shall pray for the new member of the family, and that he may be, one day, a saint in heaven, after having given his parents all possible joy and happiness on earth."

It may be thought that I multiply too much these extracts, and that these letters are not particularly interesting. For my part, I cannot help admiring the wonderful simplicity of the writer, and the total absence of all assumption of superiority over those she addresses—calling to mind how high and perfect were her virtues, and the way in which people often give severe lectures to those a little less good than themselves, in their own opinion at least. And I cannot also but appreciate that entire forgetfulness of self which always prevented her from setting herself up as an example. I like to watch her never-changing interest in her friends, at whatever distance they might be from her or however inferior in moral qualifications,—an inferiority which she alone never seemed to be conscious of.

Amongst these friends we shall often find the name of one of her relatives for whom she always had a touching and peculiar affection, and who enjoyed in the world the sort of popularity which wealth and rank secures. He seems, however, to have deserved something better than this vain and empty praise, for he appreciated and venerated his holy niece, and nothing can be more honourable to his memory than the affectionate and pious solicitude which that angelic soul felt for him to the end of his life.

Writing on the 12th of August, 1852, she says: "I have received two charming letters from Anatole Demidoff. Since I have been a Sister of St. Vincent of Paul he has sent me a beautiful rosary, and a good little sum for the poor. I cannot foresee God's designs *on* his soul, but I pray and hope much for him. I sent him a small simple image of the Blessed Virgin, which he at once accepted, and he wears it round his neck. Is not this enough to fill with gratitude a heart even more wicked than mine?"

M. Demidoff's veneration and affection for his niece never underwent a change. Whenever he came to Paris he always visited her, and gave into her hands ample alms for the poor. He had even told her to apply to him for money at all times and on all occasions. She did not trespass on his generosity, but had recourse to it sometimes with a gratitude which can be understood by those who know what an anguish it is to witness intense and pressing wants without the means of relieving them.

Natalie and the poor! M. Demidoff could not have secured for himself better friends in God's sight! They certainly never omitted to fulfil the obligations which his charity laid upon them, and acquitted their debts of gratitude by fervent prayers for him whilst he lived, and yet more earnest pleadings after his death.

CHAPTER IV.

1855—1858.

AT the beginning of 1855, Natalie had the unexpected joy of hearing that her dear and excellent friend, Marie de Bombelles, was soon coming to France. She had been residing chiefly with her father in Vienna since they had parted, and it may be easily imagined with what interest and sympathy she had watched, at a distance, the steps of the friend who was walking in the way she herself longed to tread, but in which she hardly hoped to follow her. Her health had become worse and worse, and she was so weak at that time that the least exertion was an effort, and that the slightest fatigue seemed likely to kill her. It seemed almost dangerous to let her travel; but her father, whose idol and whose only comfort she was, ardently wished to leave his adopted country and to see France once more.

Feeble as she was in body, Marie had a strong character, a courageous and devoted heart, to which nothing seemed impossible. She loved nothing on earth as much as her father, and determined, at all costs, to gratify his desire. She herself entreated him to leave Vienna, and declared that she could perfectly travel with him, and had quite strength enough for the journey. Great anxieties were felt about her, and even alarm when she started. In consequence of her feebleness it was necessary to travel so slowly that the journey to Versailles lasted a whole fortnight. But at last they arrived at that place; and there Count Charles de Bombelles fixed his residence.

It was some time before Marie recovered from the fatigue of travelling; and though so near to Natalie, had to wait a long time before she could see her. But at last they met, and we can fancy how joyful was that meeting and how sweet the converse between those friends. Marie remained, however, in the same state, and as time went on it seemed less and less likely that her health would improve. Her journeys to Paris from Versailles were generally preceded and followed by days and even weeks of exhaustion, during which she could not leave her bed. But weak and exhausted as she was, and for the most part hardly able to take food or leave her bed, she was continually occupied with her father, and devoted to him what seemed to be the last days of her existence. All at once, the Count de Bombelles was himself taken ill; his state soon became alarming, and then hopeless. From the first day of his illness, Marie rose from her bed, and sat by her father's couch day and night. Nothing could ever persuade her to leave him, and having nursed, consoled, strengthened, and supported him to the last, she saw him die in her arms.

Those who witnessed this heroic self-devotion expected to see her die also. Every one thought that her task of love once ended she would soon leave this world. But this was not to be the case,—not, at least, as they understood it. Instead of taking to her bed again, she remained better than she had been for years, eat without difficulty the food placed before her, and in fact had recovered her health so completely that no traces of her former ailments remained, or ever re-appeared. Having regained her health at the very moment when her father's death left her quite free to act as she pleased, it will not appear strange that she considered these circumstances an indication that the will of Providence was in accordance with the wishes she had felt ever since her childhood, and which in the shape of a desire, or a regret, had haunted her ever since. Nothing now opposed the realization of that wish. Her decision was soon made; and our readers will perhaps suppose that the two friends so closely united in feelings were about to have the joy not only of serving God in the same manner, but of serving Him in the same place. But this is not often the case with those who are specially called to follow the path which Marie, as well as Natalie, was now to tread. It was in the order of St. Francis de Sales, not that of St. Vincent de Paul, that she was to assume the religious habit; and, moreover, by Perè de Pontlevoy's advice, she chose as her convent home—not one of those in Paris, where she might have had a chance of sometimes seeing her friend—but one at Vienna, where her energy and zeal would find scope amongst persons she knew and could influence, and for the good of her own soul and those of others more usefully labour.

A few days before her departure from Paris, on the Feast of St. Vincent of Paul, she had a last long interview with Natalie. The two friends walked together under the beautiful trees in the garden of the Mother-house, and Marie carried away with her a never-forgotten remembrance of that conversation. No wonder that it remained impressed upon her mind and heart, for the sweetest human sympathy, much as we value it, is but a faint image of the union between souls who value each other in Christ.

Though Marie was cured, as we have said, and completely so, as the future evinced, she was still weak at the time we are speaking of, and hardly able to go through such deep and tender emotions so soon after her sufferings and agitating trials. As she returned to the house with Natalie a feeling of faintness came over her, and she had to lean against the wall in order to recover her breath. Some one who happened to be there, and saw her looking so pale and exhausted, could not help expressing surprise at the decision she had made, and asked her, "if she could not try to do good without being a nun?" "No, no!" Natalie exclaimed, "my little Sister must have the happiness of belonging entirely to our Lord."

Those words, and the way in which they were uttered, confirmed the resolution already formed by her friend, and seemed to her like a pledge that she would be able to accomplish it.

Then came the hour of separation—a separation more complete even than that which must have naturally resulted from absence, distance, and the religious life— for the two friends voluntarily and mutually gave up the pleasure of any direct communication with one another except in case of necessity. Perfectly certain that in spirit they would remain united, they determined not to correspond, and looking forward to an eternal companionship in heaven, accepted freely an entire separation on earth.

This will perhaps surprise those who do not know the ardour with which souls worthy of God's love, that which claims their whole heart, feel constrained to correspond to love by every means in their power, and to give Him all they can in return. Natalie wrote to all those, who, if they had not heard from her, would have questioned her affection. But with Marie she knew this could never be the case. In spite of all the material obstacles which separated them, they were more perfectly united than many of the most intimate friends in the world, for to love each other, and find each other, and be united one to another in God—words which seem to many mere forms of speech—were, in the case of those two souls, great and deep truths.

God rewarded their sacrifice by not accepting it in its fulness. The happiness of meeting again, which they had generously renounced, was vouchsafed to them later, for their separation when Marie left Paris did not prove a final parting.

During the years that Natalie was spending in the Secretary's department of the Mother-house her brother-in-law, the Baron de Petz, was making, as a naval officer, a voyage round the world. We have seen with what affection she mentions, in all her letters, the name of her sister's husband, and never forgets the dear, the good Tonnino. On his side, the young officer, for the sake of his sister-in-law, never omitted during his travels to visit, wherever he went, the houses of the daughters of St. Vincent of Paul. He had not, perhaps, expected to find them in all the most distant quarters of the globe, or to hear in all their convents the name and the praises of Sister Narischkin. Her zeal, her activity, her punctuality, her intelligent solicitude for each of those establishments, had endeared her everywhere to the Sisters who, many of them, had never seen Natalie, but still had been in constant correspondence with her. The Baron de Petz was surprised and touched at this universal feeling with regard to her, and she was pleased and grateful also at hearing how much kindness and respect her brother-in-law had shown to her Sisters in Religion.

Those circumstances are alluded to in Natalie's letters which we will continue to transcribe. We have noticed them beforehand in order to explain the meaning of those passages, and preclude the necessity of further explanations:

TO CATHERINE.

"*February* 26*th*, 1855.

" MY DEAR KATE,

"IF I had courage for it I should scold you very much, but I cannot find it in my heart to do so. How can you be such an age without writing me a line? I was waiting for a letter from Elisabeth, which you promised me the last time you wrote, when all at once I heard that you were both at Vienna. A line from uncle Demidoff informed me that you were going away the next day. I then relied on receiving a letter from Trieste full of interesting details, and now by one of the

13th, to Sache, I find that you are still at Vienna, and are going to remain there till the end of the week. So all my little hopes have vanished as to a letter from Trieste, and plenty of details in it. I must make up my mind to be patient. Fortunately we are in Lent, and there cannot be a more proper time for mortification and endeavours to die to oneself. The Carmelites receive no letters during Lent; our rule in this respect is not so strict, for it would not be compatible with the spirit of our Order. Scattered as we are all over the world, and occupied with universal interests—for there is not a place where we have not at heart to relieve the poor and to save souls—we are not forbidden to read letters; but now and then, in order to test our readiness to practice a little self-denial out of love for God, we carry in our pockets for two or three days a letter we had been impatiently expecting. You know that our Lord says that a glass of water given in His name will not fail to be rewarded. This leads us to hope that little acts of self-denial practised for His sake are pleasing to Him, and obtain a greater reward; for we know that to give a glass of water does not cost us much effort, but the intention with which we do the smallest acts can give them value, especially if we do not let others observe them. We must be cheerful, amiable, and cordial on every exterior occasion, and keep the rest from any eyes but His, who knows, sees, accepts and rewards everything, and without whose leave nothing can happen.

"I pitied you a little, dear Kate, during your stay at Vienna, for I think you must have been uncomfortable and bored with all those dinner parties and excursions, if indeed you were obliged to go everywhere. Did uncle Demidoff tell you that I would not consent to have my picture taken for him? Did he seem displeased at my refusal, which he must have received just at the time you were in Vienna? I want you to tell me, because he is so good that I am always afraid of vexing him, and yet it really was a request I could not agree to; I should like to know that he did not take it amiss."

TO HER SISTER ELISABETH.

"I received the other day a magnificent present of rosary beads, and recognized Kate's handwriting in the direction of the parcel; I therefore know they come from her, and I thank her with all my heart for them, but I hoped it would be followed by a little letter, which I am still expecting. Sache, who is quite a dear benefactress to us, tells me that her mother had received a letter from Kate which Tonnino brought to Naples. This gave me great pleasure, as it showed me he was nearer to you than I supposed. I do hope that by the end of another year you will have him at home again. I offered up my Communion for him the day before yesterday, and I should like to know how you all spent the day.*

Having heard this morning that the cholera is raging at Venice, I feel anxious, and I shall be particularly grateful for news of you whilst it reigns in your neighbourhood. How I wish we had sisters in that country!—but it does not seem as if they wished for us.

---

* The Feast of St. Anthony. Anthony was the name of her brother-in-law.

"I don't know what Anna Marovitch means when she writes to me that there are three houses of our Order in Venice. The little town of Lusingrande has, however, applied for Sisters. It is at twelve hours' distance from Trieste by sea. You must know about it. We answered that we should be glad to accept the offer, and the director of our house at Gratz has gone there, I think, at the request of our Superiors, to see the place and obtain more ample information. I cannot tell you how much pleased I am at this opening—not because I should expect to be one of the Sisters sent there, for I should be afraid that this would be to go out of the way assigned to me by Providence, and I never shall make an effort to obtain a change in my destination,—but I know by experience the good our Sisters do wherever they are, and that when God calls them anywhere it is to devote themselves to His glory and to the poor, and this application makes me hope that sooner or later we shall get to our dear Venice.

"Write and tell me if the cholera is very bad there, and what you are doing. Also let me know about the baths of Roitsch, and when you are to go there. Do not forget that the 3rd of July is uncle Anatole's feast. He was much pleased with a letter I wrote to him on that occasion last year. I had a charming one from him the other day all in his own hand, and when Kate sent me the beads, he added to the parcel a photograph of his mother's tomb at Pere la Chaise, which he wishes me to keep as a family souvenir. I have not yet had time to answer that letter, but I mean to do so to-day.

"When will dear little Valentine be able to read a letter? As soon as I hear that she can do so, I shall write to her. One of my companions here receives charming letters from her little niece, who is eight years old. I hope Valentine will write to me. In the mean time, my dear sisters, you must let me hear from you, particularly just now that you are in the midst of the cholera, you must not leave me without news of you."

TO CATHERINE.

"*Paris, November* 28, 1855.

"My good and dear Kate,

"I have been wishing every day to write to you since I received your little letter, which grieved me very much. I cannot understand ——'s conduct, and I suspend my judgment on that point. But it pains me to think of what you suffer, and I am surprised that the ———s do not seem to take the least heed of it. Perhaps uncle Demidoff's journey to Russia may expedite matters. I hope so with all my heart; and I will write to him when he is there, for he always receives my letters very kindly.

"I regretted very much that the Marquise Strozzi did not see you before her departure. She would have told me so many things about you that would have interested me. She gave me very sad accounts of Teresa.* How deeply tried the friends of God must always be in this world!—and how happy are those who understand that truth!

"I thought a great deal of you, dear Kate, on the Feast of St. Catharine,

---

* The Countess de Thürn.

especially whilst listening to the life of that great Saint in the Martyrology. How happy she was to suffer for God, and what courage she had! You know that she was cruelly persecuted for the faith, and that it was the generous steadfastness with which she defended Catholic truth which obtained for her the grace and glory of martyrdom. So I did not fail to recommend you to that great Saint, and earnestly to beg her to help and support you in the midst of all the difficulties, sorrows, and troubles of this life!

"Oh, if all our friends in this world would understand the advantage of suffering for God, they would not care so much for the enjoyments of life. I have sometimes heard people say something which made me tremble—that is, that our Lord, who is infinitely merciful and also infinitely just, rewards, perhaps, on earth souls which in the Divine foresight He knows will not go to heaven, and thus gives to purely human good actions the recompense they are entitled to in this world or the next. I think this is a terrible idea, and it has inclined me to quarrel with everything that gives one pleasure on earth. I do not, of course, include in this that peace of the soul and other spiritual enjoyments which are a reward granted to those who in this life are detached from everything, and deny themselves in order to follow our Lord, and at the same time are only a foretaste of those reserved for them in heaven.

"If I had an opportunity for Trieste, I would send you a book lately published which would do you good—'the Life and Works of the Blessed Henry Suso'; but you will easily get it in German. There is such a depth of knowledge in this work that one feels as if it was our Lord Jesus Christ Himself who had inspired it, and as if one was compelled to follow its teachings. But enough of so serious a subject. I have perhaps already tired you completely, dear Kate, whom I want so much to be resting in heart, in mind, and in body also, for physical suffering often reacts on both; and at this moment you are in need of strength and courage to bear with patience, and to arrive even at rejoicing over the many trials God sends you! Oh, be sure that I do not forget you in my poor prayers!—and that, above all, what I ask our Lord is, to detach you from all things, and from yourself, so that you may have no other desire but to glorify Him, whether by suffering or joy. The important thing is to arrive—to arrive at Heaven, where happiness will be eternal!

"Do not leave me very long without a few lines from you. I always think you write too seldom and too briefly; and yet I think it must do you good sometimes to 'sfogarti un poco,'* especially if nothing in your words is against charity.

"Your affectionate Sister,
"Natalie."

TO HER SISTERS.

"How I have shared your sorrow, my beloved ones!—but I feel certain that in the midst of all your trials, your hearts have been, and are still, entirely resigned. I have not heard if, since you wrote, Tonnino has been able to come home, and if he is now consoling by his presence his

---

* To open and relieve one's heart.

dear family; but I earnestly hope it may be so. You know, I suppose, that our poor uncle Anatole has been very ill. He wrote to me from Kissingen on the fifteenth of last month, and told me that he had had a second attack. I was deeply grieved at hearing it, for though trials are often merciful dispensations in the case of souls who receive them as warnings sent by God, they nevertheless forebode a sudden death, which is an awful thing for persons who are not familiarized with the thought of dying; so I am beseeching God to have mercy on that dear uncle, and I offer up all my poor little works to obtain for him a holy death in reward for his charity.

"Our director tells me that he read in the papers *that Prince Demidoff* had left*

---

* M. Anatole Demidoff had been made Prince of San Donato by the Duke of Tuscany.

Paris and returned to Germany; I cannot understand what that meant. It would surprise me very much that, ill as he was, he should have made a journey to Paris. It is probably Paul that they were speaking of. *He* does not know me, and would not be at all gratified at having a nun for his cousin. He certainly would not have knocked at the door of our community-house. But as to uncle Anatole, I do not think he would have come to Paris without letting me know, or coming to see me, if it was only because he knows what a pleasure it is to me. I bless God for the good dispositions of our dear little Valentine; these are real graces which you must try to make her correspond with, by training that little soul from her earliest years to be pious, charitable, truthful, and gentle;

and, above all things, by discouraging every tendency to vanity and self-love.

"I quite feel, dear Elisabeth, what it would have been to you to lose such a charming and dear child. And I am sure that you show your gratitude to God, who has preserved her life, by directing towards Him all the love of her little heart.

"You will be surprised to hear that I have seen several times lately poor Francis de Roussy, who has just lost his father. His wife died about a year ago, leaving him with four children. His grief was heart-rending. How many changes and sorrows everywhere! But he is as good and pious as ever, which is a great comfort. He is going to the Chateau de Sales, where his father, whom every one declares was a saint, is to be buried. He asked for your direction, and will write to you. Pray for him!—he is in need of it. And now, my dear friends, what shall I say about my poor self? Why, only that the happiness of a religious vocation is a blessing which every day I understand and appreciate more fully. I have seen that good Father Raphäel of Venice. He is now in Paris, and as good and holy as ever. He comes and talks to me sometimes of Venice, and the good Dorotheas, who also write to me now and then. There is something very sweet in this union between souls consecrated to God! We mutually encourage and help one another, and excite ourselves to become more fervent.

"Our community continues to be very flourishing. We have almost always five hundred young sisters in the noviciate. It is something really wonderful, and it seems as if it was an ark in which people take refuge. But all the religious communities are prospering and increasing just now. God appears to have special mercies in store for souls. Oh! let us bless Him for it. Thank Him also sometimes, my dear sisters, for the great favour He has bestowed on me. It is beyond what I can describe, but it will never make me love you one whit the less. I kiss my dear little Valentine, and I beg her to kiss for me her papa, her mamma, and her aunty Kate, with all the love of her dear little heart. You will tell me if she fulfils this commission.

"By-the-bye, I gave Countess Esterhazy the other day a parcel for you, in which you will find a little book called 'Lessons of the Good Angel.' It is perhaps rather too smartly bound for a present from a poor Sister of Charity, but when you give it to Valentine tell her that, later on, when she gets a purse of her own, she must give me in return an alms for the poor. This reminds me that Roussy educates so well his children in this respect, and teaches them to look upon almsgiving as a duty. One day his eldest boy was hovering about me with a little bag in which his father had put a hundred francs *for the Sister*, and he was watching for the moment to give it to me. In the most modest and prettiest way possible he came up to me and whispered, 'Sister, will you remember sometimes to pray for mamma and us?'"

TO THE VISCOUNTESS DES CARS.

"*March* 20*th*, 1858.

"You were my first thought, when I heard of the death of Father de Ravignan.

I meant to write to you, but alas! such an event is generally too quickly known; and whilst all Paris, and even all Catholic Europe, were occupied with the state of this holy religious, could I imagine that you had not heard of it? Now, the important thing for souls which had the happiness of being under his direction is, to bear in mind the wise teachings they received from him, and the lights which enabled his extraordinary and wise experience to preserve, to support, to animate, and to establish them in the firm practice of religion. How precious, dear friend, are these remembrances! Not for all the treasures of earth would we forego them, for they are indeed heavenly treasures. . .

"Think of me, dear sister, particularly on the Feast of the Annunciation; pray that it may be to me the starting-point of an entire renewal. I suppose you know that on that day the whole of our Society renew the vows made at other times of the year, and that it is our greatest festival. . .

"It would have been very ungrateful of me not to have longed and wished earnestly to tell you sooner how thankful I am for all you have done for our dear missions. How much happiness you will have given! —how many children you will have clothed in that land, once sanctified by the presence of St. Paul!—in that Damascus, once so flourishing, and now changed into a heap of ruins or turned into a receptacle of vice and misery!

"The news from China by the last mail is disastrous. Poor Kiang-si has been devastated by the rebels. The missionaries have been despoiled of everything. Sacred vessels, altar linen, and all the

Church furniture have been seized, since Christmas. Up to the time when they wrote Mass was not said owing to the want of the proper requisites for the Holy Sacrifice, and they did not know how long this sad privation would last. Poor missionaries! it is hard indeed not to have this consolation in the midst of all their trials and sufferings. It is really a bare cross that our Lord assigns them.

"At Bahia, in Brazil, the population rose against the Sisters. They have not actually been murdered, as was reported, but were struck, trodden under-foot, and dragged through the streets. Nothing could be more admirable than their feelings in the midst of all this. God be blest for it, and for giving them the spirit of Apostles. We have just lost four of them. They died like saints."

At that time accounts reached Natalie

which contradicted the hopes she had formed in consequence of M. Anatole Demidoff's considerate kindness to herself. She had fondly supposed that this respect was evinced not only towards her, but towards faith, virtue, and truth, of which the habit she was wearing was the type, and, as it were, the well-known livery. To think that this was not the case proved a severe disappointment to that pure and fervent heart, and made her deeply anxious. "Oh, how far I was from expecting what you tell me about our poor uncle Anatole! The bare idea that his poor soul may rush into such danger dismays me, and makes my blood run cold. Can one conceive such a thing in a man with one foot in the grave, and who in an instant may lose his soul for ever?—in a man whose eyes have seemed sometimes opened enough to the light of hope and truth, to make him triumph over those terrible passions which make it, alas! so hard for the rich to enter the kingdom of God! Oh, how we must multiply our prayers and supplications for him!

"I am so glad that you like 'All for Jesus,' and I shall willingly send you another copy of it. We all delight in that book. I read it in English, and found it incomparably more beautiful in the language in which Father Faber wrote it. Oh! how we must try, dear Kate, to practise everything it teaches! All for Jesus! Oh yes! —all for Him!—in life, and in death, and for a happy eternity!"

Father Etienne, the venerable Superior-General of the Sisters of Charity, always quickly discerned amidst the numerous family of which he was the head and the father, those who rose higher than the ordinary level of their holy vocation. He had soon observed the qualities and gifts with which Sister Narischkin was endowed, and though he did not indulge her, but on the contrary, as was his way when dealing with courageous souls, imposed upon her arduous and difficult duties, still he particularly cared for Natalie, and numbered her amongst his favourite children. He had witnessed her hard and unwearied labour, and perhaps noticed, though she never complained of it, that she was suffering from fatigue; and in the year 1858 he resolved to secure for her at once a little rest and a great joy. The affairs of the Order were calling him to Italy. He took Natalie to Rome with him, where she had the happiness of kneeling at the feet of Pius IX. Just at the time when she was about to enter on the last and most trying period of her life, she received that sacred and paternal blessing. Her soul had indeed by that time acquired a peace and an equality which was never again disturbed; but two trials were awaiting her which she had not up to that time experienced—a heavy responsibility in a position uncongenial to her tastes, and the gradual failure of her health and strength. Natalie was surrounded by several of her Sisters when she was received by the Holy Father, who welcomed them with his usual kindness. But after they had all bowed down again before withdrawing, Natalie remained on her knees near the seat of the Holy Father. He saw that she wished to speak to him, and bent down to listen to her.

The Sisters stood a little way off, and watched with emotion the gracious and paternal manner of the Pope, and the expression of Natalie's face whilst she knelt at his feet and raised her head to speak words to him which no one else could hear. This lasted a few minutes, and then the Holy Father smiled, gave her his blessing, and, turning to the other sisters, said, "Voilà une sainte fille," * which words gave occasion, later on, to her companions to tease the humble Sister Narischkin by telling her that the Pope had canonized her during her lifetime.

This audience was the principal event of Natalie's journey into Italy. By the side of this great privilege we can but barely mention the pleasure she felt at beholding again those fair skies which reminded her of her childhood, and also of those subsequent days when she had re-

---

* That is a holy daughter.

ceived the most vivid impressions, and formed the most important resolutions of her life.

From Rome she went to Florence, where her uncle, Anatole Demidoff, was residing. He inhabited a magnificent villa, in the vicinity of which he had founded a house of Sisters of Charity,—one amongst many other generous acts which honour his memory. His own house, called Quarto, —where after his death the Grand Duchess Marie lived—was filled twice in the course of a few years with all that wealth, and luxury, and magnificence can gather together to adorn an earthly abode; and twice also was it visited by death, which throws so awful a light on all human concerns. There was no need, in Natalie's case, of this stern monitor to make her estimate at their just rate those accumulated treasures. We can easily guess what were her thoughts and feelings during the visits she paid her uncle at Quarto. He was too ill to come to Florence, and several times she went to him. We may truly say that she entered that house like a messenger from heaven; that she was received with respect, veneration, and affection, and we may venture to hope that her holy and gentle words were not uttered in vain. It was indeed the moment for such words to find an echo in the heart of the possessor of so many earthly treasures, for he had already found out that they had given him no real happiness, and that even had they done so, they were fleeting from his grasp.

We can hardly think that those long conversations proved fruitless, or that the ardent prayers which accompanied them were not heard and granted. We cannot, indeed, affirm that such was the case, but hope and charity permit us to believe it.

It was on her way back from one of those visits that Natalie, unused to the temperature of a heated drawing-room, caught a severe cold, and felt the first symptoms of an illness which threatened to be serious at that time, and the results of which were even yet more disastrous. She was not able to return to France with Father Etienne, and it was weeks before she could travel, and at last resume her post at the Mother-house; but her health never entirely recovered that illness. Though she looked after a while much as usual, never from that time did she enjoy a single day of that full possession of physical strength which so efficiently seconds moral energy. We do not appreciate that strength till we are deprived of it, and the soul is left to act alone without the ready co-operation of the obedient and submissive slave which used so well to fulfil its biddings.

It was a little before that time that Madame Swetchine — another Russian whose name will ever be honoured and loved in France—a model of holiness, of highmindedness, and of patience in suffering, had departed this life. Those two souls, united by the same faith and the same courage—both of them an honour to the land of their birth and the country they had adopted—lived close to one another, and yet very seldom met. It was not the difference between their ages that would have stood in the way of their intimacy. The young as well as the old found in Madame Swetchine the same kindness, the same charm, the same intelligent and ready sympathy. So great was the charm of her society that it made all other companionship dull and uninteresting in comparison. But Natalie had been in Paris only a few months before she had entered the seminary, and since then her life had been concentrated in her Secretary's work. Madame Swetchine had therefore seen her but very seldom; but she watched with the most intense interest the course of her young countrywoman's courageous life, and Natalie loved and venerated her, as did all those who had ever been in communication with that chosen soul. She shared the sorrow which filled so many hearts at that irreparable loss.

It might indeed be a real subject of pride to the Russian nation—if they could arrive at feeling it—that the most perfect type of perfection of mind and heart in the life of the world, and the highest degree of sanctity in the religious vocation, were to a great degree realized in Paris, and in our days, by two of their countrywomen.

CHAPTER V.

1858.

TEN years had elapsed since Natalie had entered on the duties of the Secretaryship—ten years during which she had perfectly accomplished all her exterior duties, and made at the same time an amount of progress in the interior life which we can guess from the tone of her letters, but by no means estimate. It did not, however, escape the experienced discernment of her Superiors. They thought the time had arrived for her to occupy a post less congenial to her pious tastes and her humility, and to bear the burthen of more difficult duties and a heavier responsibility. She was far from imagining, however, what this change was to be, when one day she was sent for by Father Etienne, who in the presence of the Mother-General announced to her, not only that she was to leave the Mother-house, but also that she was going to be placed at the head of a community. She was struck dumb with surprise; not all her spirit of obedience could hide the consternation she felt at this news. It involved not only the relinquishment of her silent labours, mingled with recollection and prayer, but also that of a completely obscure and retired life such as her soul loved. This obscurity was not perhaps as complete as she imagined; but the fame which her correspondence had won for her in distant countries found no echo in the humble scene of her labours. Through her letters she was in communication with every part of the world; and yet she felt herself unknown—for in the daily habits of life nothing distinguished her from her Sisters.

At first it seemed to her that the task assigned to her was beyond her strength. Her grief and reluctance were so great that they made her almost faint away, but still she never dreamt of resisting the will of her Superiors; only, in this instance, obedience seemed to her a hard and difficult duty, and it cost her a great effort to bend her will to it. We shall see how she achieved it, and how well she justified the words of Father Etienne to the Sisters of the little community she was about to govern. He said that he was giving them *a pearl*, and that they must take great care of her; "for if you were to lose her," he added, " I should find it difficult to supply another of the same value."

The name given to the Superior of a house of St. Vincent of Paul is "Sœur Servante"—"Sister Servant"—and certainly that name was never so appropriate as in the case of Sœur Natalie. Amongst her companions there were some who could not help smiling at the idea of " the figure that dear Sister would cut at the head of the temporal affairs of a house,"—a sort of thing she had never been accustomed to; and also the fact of her being placed in authority—she who seemed able only to pray and obey, and give way to others with that humble and submissive manner which was natural to her.

To these misgivings were joined the regret at "the little Saint's" departure from the Mother-house. Her presence in what she called "that blessed Ark," had produced a never-to-be-forgotten effect, and many were the regrets which the loss of the Sœur Natalie left behind her.

"To her"—the same record relates—"it was a much greater effort to be placed at the head of fifteen Sisters than it had been to take the lowest place when she had joined the community. She continued to be as simple, as modest, and as closely united to God as before; that is indeed saying too little, for she felt more than ever that union with our Lord was the element in which she was to find strength for the multitude of duties and the wider scope of charity assigned to her."

These words describe Natalie beforehand during this new period of her life. Her occupations were changed, but to the end of her life she continued to feel a tender and ardent interest in the trials and needs of the missionaries, and to employ herself in helping them with a zeal which up to her last hour never slackened. She followed them incessantly in thought and in prayer. The trials and efforts of the Church in distant countries touched her as much as the sufferings under her own eyes, and when alms were left at her own disposal, she considered that to divide them between the poor amongst whom she lived and the missionaries who were evangelizing the heathen, was to act according to the spirit of the Gospel.

With the exception of this sympathy and participation in those Apostolic labours to which her own had been so long devoted, everything for her and about her was changed. Instead of the Mother-house with its beautiful chapel, its spacious rooms, and its large garden, she now inhabited a small house in the Rue St. Guillaume, in the parish of St. Thomas d'Aquin. And instead of the methodical and solitary life which she had been leading for ten years in the Secretary's office—a life in which every hour had its regular employment, and the same leisure always secured for meditation and prayer,—she was charged with a responsibility that obliged her to be at every moment at every one's disposal.

If, on the one hand, it was impossible that she should leave without regret her dear and delightful occupation, it would not have been in keeping with her firmness of character, her submission, or rather her love of the will of God, to look back wistfully to the past, and not to devote herself heart and soul to this new way of serving Him. Moreover, she soon found that these exterior duties did not separate her from Him in whom and for whom she lived; that to become more actively still the servant of the poor, was to be His servant in a most special sense. It is hardly necessary to describe the tender solicitude and the zeal with which she visited that large outward family, towards which she and her fifteen Sisters were to be, as it were, Mother and Sisters. This part of her duties was light and easy, but there were others which required qualities of another sort than mere devotedness.

The house in the Rue St. Guillaume, dark and narrow as it was, contained not only external classes, but also an orphanage, an infant nursery, and an asylum for old women. It had also the direction of the Bureau de Bienfaisance of that part of the town, and of several other parochial charities, each of which had its own distinct administration and budget. Some of them being entirely dependent on private support, it required a singular amount of order and foresight to manage simultaneously these various good works, and much ability and economy to make the most of their resources and keep them going. Natalie, who had thought herself even more incapable than her companions deemed her of such a task, soon, however, justified the entirely different opinion her Superiors had formed of her capabilities. Without hesitation and without haste, without presumption or over-anxiety, she went quietly to work, and was soon so well able to meet all the requirements of her new position, that as her companions said, " one would always have imagined that the only thing she had to attend to was the particular duty or occupation of the moment." And indeed, in spite of the time which so many good works absorbed, of her daily visits to the poor, and the many walks she had to take in order to relieve their wants; of the intercourse she had been obliged to renew with the families in the Faubourg St. Germain who could assist in her charities; of the particular care with which she used to seek out persons in reduced circumstances ashamed to acknowledge their poverty — in spite, I say, of so many exterior calls, Natalie never seemed absent from her post at the head of her community. The glass door of her humble little sitting-room, looking on the court, was always readily opened to all those who in their spiritual and temporal wants sought Sister Narischkin's sympathy or aid. That little room, with its straw chairs, dark-coloured walls, and common little stove, which at first sight seemed so dull and depressing, assumed a new aspect in the eyes of the poor; a brighter one than many a rich abode where they went to beg for help. Courage, consolation, and hope seemed to shine upon them in the small parlour of the Rue St. Guillaume.

Sometimes Natalie invited her visitors into what was called the Superioress's office, a small recess which could just hold her writing-table and two straw chairs, and where the interruptions were not quite so frequent as in the outer room; and it was indeed no small privilege to sit there opposite to the dear Sister, and speak with her without reserve or constraint. Sometimes without her even uttering a word, the calm and earnest expression of her countenance imparted peace to the hearts of those who sought her counsel. God only knows the number of those who entered that little room overwhelmed with heavy trouble, and who came away from it encouraged, comforted, and strengthened to bear bravely their heavy weight of care. Further on, we shall speak again of this life of intimate and intense charity, the active exercise of which was rapidly to wear out the life of Sœur Natalie; but before we proceed with our narrative, it will be well to let her describe herself some of her feelings at the outset of this last and most important period of her existence.

"*Maison de Secours, Rue St. Guillaume*, 13,
Parish of St. Thomas d'Aquin,
November 19*th*, 1858.

" It is very long since we have written to each other, and how many things, alas! have happened to me since then! The printed direction at the top of my letter will show you that I am no longer in our dear Mother-house, but in the midst of all the cares of parochial life. Pray for me, my dear friend, that I may not injure the works of God, and be so unfortunate as to prove an obstacle to the bestowal of His graces on this poor little family of fifteen Sisters, and the multitude of children who depend upon them! But oh, when shall I ever enjoy again the happiness of that hidden life which I had the happiness of leading up to this time! . . .

"I cannot, however, forget my dear missions, and my heart is still full of them; and so I hope that to comfort me a little you will think of the dear Saint whose feast we are about to celebrate on the 3rd of December.* You will not be here at that

---

* St. Francis Xavier, the Patron Saint of Missionaries.

time, but it will not signify if you authorize me to do in your name what we did other years in honour of that day.

"We have no very particular news from our foreign missions just now. At Bahia there is a very satisfactory burst of charitable feeling in every part of the town. At Lisbon everything is quieter; and the Sisters can go about more freely at St. Petersburgh. Father Souaillard (a Dominican) preaches sermons which everybody goes to hear. He was to have returned in time to preach during Advent at St. Sulpice, but they keep him at St. Petersburgh till May. Thank God for it! He knows how to make up to us for the sacrifices He requires. He alone knows how great is the one He has appointed me. My poor Sister Caille, and all my other dear companions, have felt and shared it with me. But He who has done and suffered so much for our souls deserves every sacrifice we can make. May we never refuse anything He asks of us. At this moment I feel all the bitterness of the cup, but I am determined with the most sincere will to drink it to the dregs." . . .

She surmounted all her regrets and dislikes, and soon became a perfect type of that spiritual Motherhood, which, strange as it may seem to many, has cares as sweet and joys as deep as those of mothers in the natural order. We shall see how much Natalie loved the Sisters and the children who surrounded her, and how she was in return beloved by those whom she governed with a hand as firm as it was tender. These new occupations and solicitudes did not alter in the least the simplicity of her intercourse with her relatives and friends. We only feel that the fire of love which was increasing in her heart is more and more evinced in all she writes and does. At the end of 1858, she says to her sister: "When I think of all the graces I have received, I cannot understand that love and gratitude do not entirely consume my whole being.

"It is so different to live *in the truth*, to appreciate everything according to its real worth—evil in order to fly from it, and good in order to pursue it. We then easily understand that the worldly and frivolous education so often given in the world has no other object than that of stimulating self-love, and makes it almost impossible not to make shipwreck over and over again. How many tokens of mercy I have received, and how gratuitously they were bestowed on a poor creature who spent her life in offending God! I feel it so much since I have dwelt in the hollow of the rock, —the blessed refuge of God's house. Oh, what would I not give that every one could see things in their true light!"

In the month of August, 1860, she wrote to the Viscountess Des Cars the following touching narrative: "You know, perhaps, by this time, how merciful the God of St. Vincent of Paul has been to our Sisters at Damascus, where, at nine o'clock in the evening, Abdel Kader's Algerines arrived at the door of their house to save them. They were preparing for martyrdom, and receiving the Holy Viaticum. The missionaries had been all day engaged in hearing the confessions of the Sisters and the children. They all thought that they were doomed to a certain death, and at first were almost afraid to open the door, and it was only by dint of knocking and encouraging cheers that those good Algerines reassured them and obtained entrance. Unfortunately, they could only carry them away by detachments; the last had to wait till eleven o'clock, in dreadful alternations of hope and fear. When the Emir's son came to fetch them the Turks were so near that five minutes later it would have been too late to save the Sisters. As soon as they had left it, their poor little house was invaded and destroyed. They beheld this sad devastation. Nothing was saved but their lives, and they heard the words uttered, 'Here they are, let us kill them.'

"Fortunately they were well escorted, and after an hour and a half of painful and toilsome walking over the ruins, they at last arrived at a place of shelter, quite exhausted in body and in mind. They were received with the greatest kindness and sympathy. What can we say to our Lord in gratitude for such an escape! We feel at such moments as if our hearts were too small; and a wish to expand and extend them in every direction. Help us to thank God!"

"*Paris, Feast of St. Andrew*, 1860.

"I have to inform you of the martyrdom of Father Gaëtano Massa, which happened in China in the month of August. How many graces have been granted to that family! It is from one of our Lazarist Missionaries that we heard this event. He says in his letter: 'This Father, the fourth in his family who embraced the Apostolic life, arrived in Kiang-Nam only to die a violent death. The fifth son was lately delivered by our troops. He had been captured by pirates, and was threatened with the same fate as his brother. The mother of these five heroes of charity has left the world, we hear, and retired into a cloister.' These details showed me at once that this martyr was my dear Father Gaëtano,* whom I knew had gone back to China. I cannot tell you with what joy I now invoke him! If the world is silent as to all these things, in heaven we shall hear of the glory of these blessed souls!"

"*August*, 1862.

"I heard yesterday that on the 4th Madame Obrescoff died quite suddenly. I have been deeply grieved at this news. She had just arrived at Vichy alone, with her maid, and that very night she expired. Pray for her as I shall do as long as I live. She was so kind to me. I have reasons to

---

* One of the friends of her childhood at Sorrento.

be grateful to her which I can never forget.*

"I do not know if you will be able to read this scrawl, but the children frightened me so much just now that I am trembling all over. They screamed so dreadfully that I ran up-stairs terrified, and found—what do you think?—that a mouse was running under the table. That was indeed an event to throw a whole house into agitation! Every one who heard those piercing screams was of course alarmed. What a courageous set of little girls we have!

"I have to thank you for your gifts, which could not have arrived at a better moment than the eve of New Year's Day.

---

* It was this excellent friend who had taken Catherine and Natalie to Brussels, in 1843, on the day of Olga's death.

Now that I am the Mother of so large a family you can easily fancy how doubly acceptable is everything which enables me to give pleasure to my children—only I had not time to write. I have been, and am still, suffering from a stitch in the side, which has confined me to my bed for several days, and even now a large plaster on my right side will not allow me to wear our habit; so I cannot dress, but I can write, as you see, which shows you I am much better.

"Try to find out for me, dear Kate, where L—— is now. She once told me that she meant to adopt a child. When she said this to me I had none of my own, but now that I possess seventy children I should like to remind her of this wish. By-the-bye, as you ask me if I am reconciled to my new position, I will tell you with the most perfect sincerity that it is God's will to make it abound with consolations, though they are mixed with some thorns. If it was not for the weight of responsibility all would be well. But if you knew what it is to feel that I have to answer for so many souls entrusted to my care! We are fifteen Sisters here, amongst whom there is one much older than myself. The object is to make them all find obedience easy and sweet, and then to watch over the temporal and spiritual welfare of everybody—of our old women as well as of our young people, who with the day scholars and the girls of the Patronage are three hundred in number.

"But I cannot describe to you the consolation these children gave me the day of their first Communion, and during the retreat which preceded it, by their recollection and piety. It was really too delightful to say the Rosary with them in their work-room. They had excellent instructions; and the rest of the time was spent in pious reading, manual work in silence, meditation, and singing hymns. On the day of the first Communion, our poor little orphans sang, accompanied by the organ, in such a very pious and charming manner that everybody was astonished. But pray a great deal for me. Responsibility is a heavy burthen!"

On the 10th of September, 1860, she heard of the death of the Vicomte Des Cars, and wrote the following letter to the dearest of her friends in that her hour of sudden and terrible bereavement:

"I have just heard of the affliction which has befallen you, and it awakens in the depth of my heart the feelings of a sister and of a friend. I wish I was with you, that you might feel it; but I know that earthly consolations are nothing to you now. You are impelled to seek them there where it is right to look for them, and where they can never fail you. Oh, what a day in which to suffer!—that of the Nativity of Mary— of Mary born for suffering, and who could not see a heart dearer to her learning on this day what she understood so well all through her life! Yes, dear friend, she will help you to carry this heavy cross. . . . Accept it with courage; and by her intercession may Jesus make you feel that to suffer with Him is better than all the joys of this world. You have always understood it; but there are times when the soul is overcome, and that is why I beseech our Lord to be your support and strength. You must remember that you are a mother, and that your children have a double claim upon you now."

A few months afterwards it is the affliction of friends, always so dear to her, which fills her heart with sorrow:

"Françoise de Maistre * yielded up her beautiful soul to God on the 29th of July, at Beaumesnil, where her family live. I have the happiness of seeing every year one or another of those dear and holy people,— sometimes the Count, sometimes one of his brothers. Madame de Terray comes the oftenest. The day before yesterday it was dear Marie who was with me; she grows more and more holy, and each time I see her I am more edified. I heard from her all the particulars of Frances' pious death, for she arrived ten days before at Beau-

---

* The daughter of Count Rodolph de Maistre.

mesnil. What a blessing it is to live as a Saint, seeing we die as we have lived! Marie told me also some edifying things about Xaverine; young as she is, and always in pain, she is by her words and her example quite an apostle, and like a little St. Catherine of Sienna,—by her fervour and the zeal for the glory of God which burns in her heart.* The De Maistres established a few years ago, at Beaumesnil, a house of our Sisters. I know some of them, and when they come to Paris I am quite in admiration at all they tell me of that dear family, with whom they are in constant communication.

* We may add here what she wrote in 1862: "Xaverine de Maistre has entered a Carmelite Convent. Her generous parents have made this sacrifice, like so many others,.with the greatest courage. They are alone now, but heaven, which they are looking to, will be their reward for all they have given to God."

"My faithful Sister Barba is still very fond of me, and helps me very much. She came to see me yesterday, and brought me some barley-sugar because they had told her I coughed a good deal."

This incessant cough, and that stitch in the side which she mentions in one of her preceding letters, were, alas! slowly but surely undermining her strength. It was only by dint of constant efforts that she accomplished her numerous and fatiguing duties. But for a long time she concealed the amount of those efforts, and only smiled when she was questioned about her health.

Natalie was not afraid of suffering, and still less of dying. But she was content to live in the enjoyment of obedience and activity, and her soul enjoyed all the elements of that peace which the world has no conception of. To love life, to be happy to die, and not to dread suffering, is not that real happiness?—and is not a soul thus blest armed at all points?

CHAPTER VI.

1858.

IMPERFECTLY as we have hitherto accomplished our task, the readers of this biography have been able to follow the course of Sœur Natalie's life, and to form some idea of the successive developments of her soul. But in the same way as the difficulty of ascending a mountain goes on increasing as we approach the summit, so do we find more and more difficulty in writing this narrative as we draw near to the end of an existence, every step of which was an ascension. At this point of our work, we would fain call upon that dear soul—now delivered as it is from every fear, and especially that of pride, which she had so great a dread of—and beg of her to help us not to praise her, but to praise that God whom she so much loved, and to describe so that it may be understood that mysterious spiritual transfiguration so impossible to realize humanly speaking, and yet such an admirable subject of contemplation even for those to whom it is not given to approach the sublime heights where it is consummated. How often, whilst dwelling on those touching recollections, has our heart ached and our eyes filled with tears, as we thought of the hatred which seeks beforehand to influence popular passions against these friends of the poor, of the people, and of the countries where, at this very moment, they are pursued, persecuted, banished, and forced to seek a shelter in distant lands across the ocean—that cruel ocean which not long ago swallowed up in its billows, as merciless as their enemies, several of those pure and innocent victims.* These are thoughts which would disturb the mind and embitter the soul were it not that the whole of Christianity is founded on the idea of a Divine union between innocence and suffering, and that it promises an inestimable efficacy to all sacrifices offered up in union with the great sacrifice of the Divine and heavenly victim.

In the last chapter we gave a simple

---

* On the 7th of December, 1875, five poor nuns, driven out of the Convent of Saltzrothen, in Westphalia, were drowned on their way to America, not far from the coast of Ireland. The vessel perished with all on board. The victims of the cruel laws now persecuting the Catholics of Germany, were—Barbara Hultenschmidt, Henrica Fasbænder, Norberta Reinhover, Aurea Badzinz, and Briggitte Damhorst.

outline of the various duties to which Sister Natalie devoted all the energies of a strong will and an ardent charity, which up to nearly the end of her life continued to supply the place of the strength which was gradually failing her. By means of a number of documents in our hands, we will describe with greater detail this last period of her life, and show what she was in her daily intercourse with her Sisters, with the children under her care, with her friends; and, as far as may be permitted to our weakness to penetrate into the intimate sanctuary of her soul,—with God Himself.

The revolutionary hurricane which for nearly a hundred years has raged with more or less long intervals in France, has not spared, at times, the Sisters of St. Vincent of Paul, though it has often happened that the simple good sense of the people proved sufficient to protect them against the efforts of a senseless malignity. One might even go so far as to say that it is rather the fashion to except them from the general attacks on Religious Orders—an exception which they would be the first to protest against, were they aware of the fact. But they are for the most part unconscious of the abuse lavished on their cloistered Sisters, and of the praises which worldly people,—who fancy that to pray like the Carmelites is to do nothing, and that to work like the Sisters of Charity is not in itself a prayer,—are ready to bestow on their own vocation. It has been indeed wisely said, "that there are people whom their enemies cannot safely come into contact with, if they want to go on hating them." It is therefore natural that the opportunities of seeing and knowing the

Sisters of Charity, which result from the duties of their vocation, should have tended to disarm enmity and soften animosity, which abstract arguments would never have overcome.

If this is true with regard to all the Sisters of St. Vincent of Paul, it especially applies to those who are appointed to govern their communities. It has often struck me that if a great assembly was called together for the express purpose of bestowing special honours on women who possess the manly gifts of wisdom, intelligence, discernment, and courage, and at the same time carry to the highest pitch the virtues peculiar to their sex—piety, purity, charity, and self-devotion—the foremost in merit, the first in rank, amongst those chosen souls would be the holy and valiant band of those women—the mothers, the sisters, and the guides of their companions—and who have attained, I am not afraid of saying so, not only the height of Christian virtue, but also that feminine perfection the idea of which they alone fully realize.

Sister Natalie had her appointed place amongst those chosen souls. In that house of the Rue St. Guillaume, which she so admirably governed for seventeen years, it is impossible not to feel, that in spite of its unattractive appearance there is a lingering perfume of sanctity which speaks of the holy influence so long pervading it. We find there not merely a community retaining the pious remembrance of a venerated superior, but a sorrowing family mourning over the irreparable loss of a beloved mother. As soon as Sœur Natalie's name is mentioned, the faces of all the Sisters reveal their tender affection for their late Superior, and volumes could be written full of the details they so lovingly relate.

As it is impossible to transcribe all these touching reminiscences, we shall draw from them the best picture we can of that young and humble Superior who assumed the reins of government with so much dread and reluctance, and who contrived to hold them with such a firm and gentle hand.

Sister Natalie knew so perfectly how to obey, that in spite of all her humility she could not but admit the fact, that never once during the ten years she had spent in the Secretary's office at the Mother-house had she failed with regard to that virtue. But at the same time she possessed all the requisite qualities for the government and direction of others. Together with an exact observance of the holy rule of her Order, and a spirit of mortification which made her treat her body with the utmost contempt, she ever preserved that sweet and attractive gentleness which, as by a spell, led on others to perfection, and prevented her ever appearing too austere. But this characteristic sweetness, which gave her so singular an influence over the children as well as the Sisters under her care, did not interfere with the firmness which when necessary she knew how to evince. Her countenance on these occasions commanded instant respect. One of her companions said that she would rather have performed the severest penance than have seen those eyes, so sweet in their usual expression, fixed upon her with severity. Reproofs, however, were seldom necessary. Sister

Natalie inspired her companions with that desire of perfection which filled her own soul, and next to the happiness of having fulfilled a duty, they knew no greater joy than that of pleasing their dear Superior. They watched her countenance in order to make sure that nothing in their manners, their words, or their acts, had disturbed its sweet equanimity, for Natalie took to heart the least imperfection in their conduct, and the suffering it caused her was visible in her face.

But notwithstanding this holy strictness, nothing could exceed her tenderness and kindness to those for whose perfection she was so keenly solicitous, not only in the daily habits of their common life, in which she herself was always a model of amiability, but in every possible respect. In whatever sorrow they had to endure, whether spiritual trials or anxieties, or grief with regard to their families, no mother could have shown a more affectionate, intelligent, and persevering sympathy. Nothing which interested them was ever indifferent to her. They could always command the resources of her acute and clear mind, and the warm feelings of her heart. Indeed, when any one has seen the treasures of a heart given to God poured forth in their rich abundance, it almost provokes a smile to hear people of the world claim a monopoly of deep affections.

In the midst of this influential position, Sister Natalie's modest manners never changed. One of her companions relates, that having been sent from a house in the provinces to the Mother-house, in order to proceed from thence to the one of the Rue St. Guillaume, she met there a gentle, humble-looking Sister who offered to show her the way to her future home. The offer was accepted, and also that of making over her bundle to her companion, who carried it all the way. It was only when they arrived that the new-comer found out that it was her Superior whom she had treated in so free-and-easy a manner. Feeling much ashamed she began to beg her pardon, but Sœur Natalie stopped her excuses by such a hearty burst of laughter that the young sister was obliged to laugh also; and this leads us to speak of a peculiarity in her character which will complete the picture we are trying to draw. This was a frank, ready, and expansive merriment,—a quality which we have often remarked in persons broad in mind and pure in heart. Sister Natalie's companions tell us, that "if she heard or noticed something funny, it made her laugh so that she was obliged to hold her sides and cry for mercy." This merriment, the involuntary and spontaneous result of the interior joy which overflowed her soul, was totally unlike the laughter too often excited in worldly people by levity of thought and ill-natured ridicule. Sœur Natalie would have wept at what makes such persons laugh; but where nothing of that sort was in question she manifested a child-like gaiety, "which, when it arises from purity of heart and a serene life, outlives grief, and re-appears after stormy hours like the sunshine of a soul at peace." *

These words, applied with truth to others in former days, are even more strongly applicable to her whom I am describing—one who had been severed so early

---

* "A Sister's Story."

from earth's troubles and cares, and who was enjoying a foretaste of eternal peace.

Children were peculiarly sensible to the charm of Natalie's endearing qualities. They are gifted, generally speaking, with a sort of supernatural perception. Has not our Lord said of those little ones, "their angels in heaven always see the face of my Father;"* and may we not suppose that those same angels inspire them with a secret attraction for souls which more particularly reflect the Divine image? Be that as it may, Sister Natalie inspired a wonderfully devoted and strong affection to her little charges, and exercised an extraordinary influence over all young people. Her words, her example, the manner in which she knew how to praise and encourage them, the way in which

---

* Matt. xviii. 10.

she wisely guided their consciences, were all animated by that true charity to which God concedes—as well as to faith—the power of working miracles. A number of young girls thus grew up under her wing to whom she proved a guardian angel. From the work-room of the Rue St. Guillaume they went forth in various directions, and are now living in the midst of that immense and dangerous Paris, so full of snares for youth and poverty—those true children of Sister Narischkin, as they love to call themselves—they continue in their various positions to do honour to the memory of their Mother, by their persevering fidelity to her teachings, and the promises they made to her.

Amongst a number of other instances, I will quote the testimony of a young seamstress who, when she heard of the work we are engaged in, sent us the letters she had received from her whose humble child she had been, and expressed her love for that dear Mother with a simple and touching eloquence:

"Nothing that I could say to you, Madame," she wrote, "would describe what she was to me. She was my Mother, that is all I can say! and such a Mother!—the Mother of my heart! How she watched over me in the difficult days of early life! How anxious she used to get if she lost sight of me—she who had so much else to think of! Once, she burnt for me, during a whole fortnight, the lamp which she used to light at the foot of the image of our Lady of Lourdes; and now that she is in heaven, I feel the unmistakeable effects of her protection. Oh! how I go on loving that dear Mother! I will always lead a good life so as to deserve to meet her hereafter."

We will also transcribe one of the letters which that good Mother wrote in return to her child. It will show the way in which she had set about winning her heart:

"My dear little P——,

"As I do not know your new direction, which you have been giddy enough not to give me, I delayed a little answering your letter. But I think with your name, and a good hunt in the house of the Rue St. Guillaume, that they will be able to find you out. If not, so much the worse; the letter will be returned to the postman with *unknown* written upon it. Oh, what a blessing it would be if you could be indeed *unknown* to creatures and known only to God! Do not you think so, dear child? Have an ardent wish to know Him. Apply yourself earnestly to this great and useful science, and your time will be well spent, whether you are washing the plates, or employed in the kitchen, or busy in the great work-room, or yet again at St. Cloud. Wherever you are, and at all times, keep your heart fixed on the Heart of Jesus. Be occupied with Him, and with efforts to please Him. You know what our Lord said to one of His faithful servants—St. Gertrude, I think, or St. Catherine of Sienna—' Think of Me, my daughter, and I will think of thee.' It is sweet indeed to feel that Jesus thinks of us, and we can have that perfect conviction, my dear child, and cherish and foster it in our souls—for there is only one condition attached to it, and that condition is in our own power.

" Thank you for your good prayers for

me, the effects of which I am conscious of. Go on praying for me, and believe me always yours in Christ,

"SISTER NARISCHKIN."

Another day she writes to the same young girl a long letter, which ends thus:

"I have nothing to send you to-day except a kiss in honour of the feast of your holy patron, and earnest and sincere wishes that you may daily increase in holiness. . . . I think I shall be at home again at the beginning of next week. You will then pay me a visit, and *tête-à-tête* in my room you will tell me all your little troubles with that simplicity which I always find and so much like in you, and if you need a little bit of a scolding I shall be sure to give it. Come now, dear child of our good God, have then a little courage, and with His grace and a really good will, you will do everything you ought. Give up everything rather than lose everything. You understand what I mean; and you will be sure, won't you, to come and see me on Sunday? I shall expect you.

"Your affectionate and devoted

"MOTHER."

A few days afterwards, she says:

"God be praised, my very dear child! I was anxiously awaiting this little word from you. Your silence made me uneasy. I am pleased with you, my dear. Be always thus frank and open with your Mother, and God will bless you. The little lamp is still burning for you. . . . Pray for me."

This young girl had left the work-room of the Rue St. Guillaume at the age of twenty-one, and in one of the most noisy parts of Paris was employed in a house of business, where she earned enough to support her mother and herself. Every night she brought home her earnings to the humble lodging in the suburbs where they lived together, and thus had to walk to and fro each day through the crowded thoroughfares of the gay city. Many were the temptations and snares in her way, and she could have pleaded the excuse of poverty so often urged by those who fall into sin—for it was only hard and incessant toil that preserved her from destitution. She has had, however, the will and the grace to remain worthy of the Mother and friend whose memory continues to support and strengthen her.

At the same time as we pay this tribute to the humble and courageous virtues of this dear child of Sister Natalie's, we cannot refrain from congratulating the large number of young persons in a similar rank of life, who tread the same path, and give the same example in the midst of all the temptations of Paris. May God bless them and the devoted women whose vigilant watchfulness protects and befriends them! We may hope that these pure courageous hidden lives will avert some of the judgments which sooner or later overtake scandalous sins. They are, at any rate, a consolation to those who behold, with aching hearts, the mad career of so many girls of the same rank, but not protected in the same way, who are rushing forward in idleness, unbelief, and pride, towards the future abyss which awaits them!

In Sœur Natalie's letters, which we have already quoted, her faithful and tender attachment to her friends has been so often evinced that it seems superfluous to revert to it again. We wish, however, to point out that amongst all these affections, none are more conspicuous than those relating to her native land, from which she was in a double manner separated. Nothing regarding Russia was ever indifferent to Sister Natalie. Her heart, otherwise so free from human cares, was always moved by anything which concerned the country of her birth; and when, later on, the cholera broke out in St. Petersburgh, we shall see the feelings with which her charity and her love for Russia inspired her.

This patriotic feeling, so strong in that country, increased in this chosen soul in proportion as her growth in holiness and the clearness of her views enabled her to understand better the past and the present, and to look forward to the future. She saw that all which the Greek Church had given her in the days of her childhood and youth had been confirmed and expanded by the teachings of the Catholic Church, and completed by the religious life. The dogmas she had always received with faith she now held in a more firm manner, since she believed in the visible seat of an invisible authority. Those two Churches made to be one were separated, and so separated that had she appeared in Russia in her religious garb she would have been amenable to the laws. The Christian progress her soul had made, placed her in her own country under a ban, and stamped her as an alien. . . . Was this just?—was it logical? No; but such was the fact, and if by shedding her blood Sister Natalie could have made it otherwise—we are not speaking at random when we assert that—she would gladly have done so to the last drop.

When Father Schouwaloff, her countryman, and like herself a convert to the Catholic Faith and a member of a Religious Order, gave a definite form to this desire; when an association of prayer was formed to second his efforts, and that he invited every Catholic heart to join in it—not one of them responded with more ardour to this appeal than Sister Natalie. This intense desire to propagate the truth, natural to all converts, is more peculiarly strong in those from the Greek Church. The idea of seeing the fatal barrier which separates the Eastern from the Western Church disappear; the hope of hearing them both called by the single appellation of *the Church*—these are thoughts which inspire the heart of every Russian Catholic with an ardour of desire which it is difficult for others to understand.

Nothing more illogical and contradictory can be conceived than the attempts of union sometimes talked of in these days between the Greek Church and Protestant Churches and sects. Even before her conversion Sister Natalie's clear intellect perceived the impossibility of such an alliance. The simplest power of reflection would seem sufficient to show that the Greek Church, if it united itself with the Catholic Church, would preserve unbroken the traditions of her venerable antiquity as well as the dogmas she holds; and that, ceasing to be local, she would recover that power of expansion and evangelization which she has so entirely lost from the time that schism paralyzed and isolated her. In that case she could be compared to a Princess of high birth who resumes her position in a Royal family from which she had been long separated.

But to ally herself with Protestantism would be indeed the worst of *mésalliances*—the wilful abdication of all the rights derived from a long line of illustrious ancestors.

After Sister Natalie emerged from the obscurity of the Secretary's office at the Rue du Bac, and was more known to the public, it was not only her countrymen and her old friends who sought her out, but a number of persons—strangers to her up to that time—who, attracted by the charm of sanctity combined with natural gifts, came to ask her for advice and consolation amidst the various sufferings of life. The multitude of these visitors would have been very oppressive if she had not possessed the talent of shortening useless conversations, and devoting all the leisure she could spare from her daily duties to those who repaired to her under the pressure of real sorrows and difficulties. In the most polite and amiable manner possible she knew how to keep at a distance, without offending them, those who had no such claim on her time.

A woman of the world once said, "I am very fond of that young Superior, and only to look at her does me good; but I never go and see her without necessity, for I feel she is an interior person who does not like to lose her time in conversation."

An interior person! Oh, yes; our dear Sister Natalie, in spite of the multiplicity of her external duties, did indeed lead an interior life; the spirit of Martha and that of Mary were never more blended in one person than in her who from her earliest youth had felt this double attraction. The very sound of her voice added to the effect of the words she uttered, and imprinted them in the mind with a strange power,—they seemed like the echo of that Divine interior voice in her soul. One day that I was sitting with her in the little room I have already described, enjoying a conversation which combined the charm of an intimate friendship with the useful effect of something approaching to a confession, she made an answer to one of my observations which I have never forgotten. Speaking in a foolish manner, but common enough to those who are mere beginners in the spiritual life, I said, "It is not very difficult to detach oneself from earth, but what is awful is the thought of even a happy eternity,—of something unknown." She looked surprised, and clasping her hands together exclaimed, "Oh! it is possible that you can call Heaven something unknown!"

The way in which she said those words

was in itself a sermon, or rather a revelation, for they made me feel a blessed consciousness of nearness to a soul which had soared so much higher than my own into the region of truth and light. We cannot repeat it too often—even if we have not the strength to scale the heights of perfection ourselves, it is good and useful to listen to those who dwell on those summits.

Sister Natalie, whose hand was so light and so dexterous in dressing the wounds of the poor and ministering to sufferers in their sick-beds, had also a singular gift for soothing aching hearts and healing their woes. We cannot number the friends she made during that last period of her life, the temporal sufferings which her wise and practical spirit enabled her to relieve, the moral trials of every sort which her penetration knew how to discern. No kind of misery escaped her pitying care, even those which the world does not compassionate. We are not alluding to those sad falls which it brings about with such deceitful snares and afterwards condemns with such relentless cruelty; we mean those sorrows which proceed from infirmity of character, and which draw forth the remark, "So much the worse if such persons suffer; it is their own fault if they choose to be unhappy:" or, "Others in their position would consider themselves fortunate:" or again, "They are a torment to themselves and everybody else:"—and all those kind of observations which are intended to absolve those who utter them from the troublesome necessity of pitying those to whom they refer. Very different was the holy charity of the heart so closely united to the Sacred Heart—the only perfect and Divine furnace of boundless love. We cannot indeed number those who looked up to Sister Natalie with the tenderness children feel for a mother, and the trust which sanctity inspires.

There is, however, one amongst her friends whom we must mention, for she had a very particular share in Sister Natalie's affectionate solicitude. The Countess of —— had been very intimate with Marie de Bombelles; and when the latter withdrew within the walls of the Visitation, her grief was so great that a judicious friend confided to Natalie's tender heart the task of comforting and supporting her. This proved one of those blessings which those alone can understand to whom God has sent in the hour of their utmost need an arm to support them, a voice to encourage, and a heart to love them. No wonder that these blessings were reciprocated with grateful affection. The Comtesse de N——, who did not live in France, used to make at stated periods a long journey in order to visit her whom she called the benefactress of her soul. She used to bring her children to Sister Natalie, who kept them whole days with her own little flock. Their mother lodged close to the convent, in order to spend as much time as possible in the little parlour of the Rue St. Guillaume. The immense and luxurious city of Paris was comprised for her in that humble little house in a neglected corner of the Faubourg St. Germain, far from the eyes of the aristocratic world of that fashionable locality, and all but unknown to the inhabitants of the other bank of the Loire.

Long absences intervened between these short meetings, but Sister Natalie's letters supplied the void of actual separation. In the midst of the daily occupations we have enumerated she found means to perpetuate salutary influences by a regular correspondence. Time as well as money multiplies in the hands of those who know how to employ them, and Natalie could always command both when there was question of showing sympathy or of distributing alms.

CHAPTER VII.

1865.

IF we have found it difficult to describe the details of Sister Natalie's active life, and still more all her friendly and charitable intercourse with others, what will it be if we now attempt to fathom the depths of her soul, and penetrate the main-springs of all her virtuous actions. We should not have ventured on a task so much beyond our ability, and for which we might justly be deemed incompetent, had we not been enabled to adduce testimony of incontestable weight and importance.

She used to say herself, "To love Jesus Christ, to possess Him, to adore Him, to rest on His Sacred Heart, is heaven on earth, and all this we can do at the foot of the Tabernacle. But it is still too imperfect; I want heaven with its light, and to be never separated from the Heart of Jesus."

These few lines tell us what she possessed and what she longed for. They sum up all that we could learn on so delicate and intimate a subject from those whose mission it was to follow and to second her in its last and most perfect development.

From the outset of her life Natalie had always been humble and sincere. But in proportion as her horror of the least imperfection increased, she became more and more severe towards herself; and if in the sunlight of her soul she discovered the least particle of earthly dross, it became an imperative need and an inexpressible relief to accuse herself, to humble herself, and to manifest the most secret recesses of her conscience. " The bare idea that the least atom in the pure heaven of her soul might escape the eyes of her spiritual guide was a strange suffering to her." Such were the words of one of those most familiar with Natalie's hidden life—of one who confirmed all we have said of her natural tendencies to perfection and the fidelity with which she abandoned herself to the influences of grace,—and who has made known to us more than anybody else the greatness of her soul, the generosity of her character, and its firm energy, —qualities which, in hearts closely united to God, do not deteriorate from their simplicity or their humility.

Natalie showed in every way this

generous-heartedness. Nothing could, indeed, exceed the strict economy she practised, the perfect order of everything about her, or the austere poverty which her example inculcated; still she liked to spend generously, and almost lavishly, the alms which those who had full confidence in her left in her hands. Far and wide did her bounty extend, not only with regard to her dear missions, but all the wants of the Church. She seemed to stand aloft, if we may use that expression, and to look far beyond her immediate circle for the objects of her charity. She was, as we have seen, prodigal of her affection as well as of her alms; but if such was the case towards those to whom she was united on earth by the ties of sympathy, compassion, and charity, what shall we say of her love of Him whom she loved with a love exceeding all earthly affection?—for Him for whom, the same witness tells us, she yearned with all the most intense longings of her soul—Him who was the supreme and blessed end of her desires—the ocean of all beauty, goodness, love, and wisdom, in whose immensity she would fain have plunged and assuaged the burning thirst of her soul. This desire often amounted to a keen suffering; and she might truly have applied to herself the words of St. Augustine, "Irrequietum est cor meum, Domine, donec requiescat in te." *

The gift of unitive prayer, with which God often favours those souls who desire to devote themselves wholly to Him, had been amply bestowed on Sister Natalie. She could remain for hours without fatigue kneeling before our Lord in the Blessed

---

* St. Augustine's Confessions, Bk. I., ch. 1.

Sacrament, and it was only by a strong effort she could tear herself away. Her spiritual guide had to interfere on that point with her devotion, and warn her of the danger of forgetting the lapse of time in that Sanctuary where she often and so fervently offered herself as a victim to disarm the wrath of God, and to obtain for others the grace to know and love Him.

Instead of finding a difficulty like most other people to place herself in the presence of God, and to banish the thoughts of external things, Sister Natalie was constrained to make efforts to resist the attraction which forced her, as it were, towards the Tabernacle, where she adored her God really present.

But after being placed on her guard against yielding to the temptation of prolonging her prayer, to the neglect of other duties, she never gave way to it again. It was observed that, on the contrary, however absorbed she was in contemplation, the moment any one called her she rose and left the chapel. Once only, in the case of a visit which she knew to be unimportant, Sister Natalie sent word that she was engaged. She afterwards reproached herself for that answer, fearing that she had failed in charity.

But when there was no obstacle to her remaining before the Altar, she was wont to abide there in a state of such deep recollection, that she neither saw nor heard anything that went on about her. A person who went one day into the chapel to speak to Sister Natalie, relates that as she opened the door she saw her kneeling without support in the middle of the little oratory, with her eyes fixed on the Tabernacle. Her countenance expressed the deepest peace and serenity. She seemed to be gazing on her God through the visible veils which concealed Him from her. The visitor did not venture to advance, afraid of interrupting that holy soul's intercourse with our Blessed Lord, and remained for a long time standing at the door, fascinated and riveted by that wonderful sight.

It would indeed have been a pity if Natalie had not readily complied with the summons of those who interrupted her prayers, for when she had been spending some time—as she expressed it—near that sacred fire, there was something so holy about her appearance that it seemed to impart to those who saw her a knowledge and an appreciation of true goodness. It was this we are told by a venerable missionary priest, who often had conversed with her, which made it so profitable to the soul to be in communication with Sister Narischkin. It was impossible not to feel oneself growing better whilst conversing with her; her soul was so full of the love of God that it emitted the odour of sanctity St. Paul speaks of. Wherever she went she carried with her the presence of Jesus Christ, and communicated to others that holy and sacred impression.

It is easy to understand that the result of so intense a love of God was an ardent desire to leave this world, and so keen a longing for heaven that it sometimes deprived her of *the patience to live.* The same person adds, "I have never seen in any one to such a high degree the feeling of St. Paul, 'Unhappy that I am, who shall deliver me from the body of this death?'" *

---

* Rom. vii. 24.

The wise director of her conscience thought that she sometimes carried this desire to an inordinate degree, and reminded her of St. Martin's words on the threshold of his eternal home, "Non recuso laborem." This ardent longing for death did not proceed in Natalie from the wish to be delivered from the sufferings of life. She expressed and felt the greatest indifference as to what her body might have to suffer, and the sequel proved that these words were not in her mouth vain expressions. Detachment from the world and a desire for heaven were, on her part, acts of pure and perfect love of God, and proceeded from the wish to love Him still more perfectly. They were another instance of the feeling known only to Saints, and which has made them exclaim, "I die of not being able to die;" and fills them in the midst of their sufferings with a mysterious joy so overpowering, that it forces them to cry out, "Enough, enough, my God!"

We have shown how much good Natalie did to others. We will now say a few words of the good that others did to her. The Jesuits she always looked upon as her first Fathers. Father Aladel had guided her steps in the path of the Saints. We know what Father Etienne thought of her whom he called "a pearl," and of his happy influence over her. We should have liked to name those who were her last directors, and particularly Father Chinchon, who led her to the very summit of perfection, and for whom she had an extraordinary reverence. But we have not time to speak of all these friends of her soul, and must limit ourselves to a brief mention of those whom a providential inspiration attracted to the little convent which they frequented for a while, receiving, and in return giving, singular edification.

Amongst these pious visitors we find Father Hermann, whose conversion had so very much touched Sister Natalie. She was never tired of perusing the affecting account he wrote of the wonderful grace vouchsafed to him. We have seen with what joy she welcomed the appearance of this holy religious at the Mother-house, where he came to say Mass one day whilst she was there.

In 1862, he spent a fortnight in Paris, and every day during that time he said Mass in the little chapel of the Convent in the Rue St. Guillaume. A direct and intimate communication then began between two souls well-fitted to understand each other. But nothing we could say will describe this as well as the following letter from Sister Natalie to her sister Catherine:

"How can I thank you enough for your generous gift? It is in your name that I shall assist the good works your charity enables me to promote. I, who am poor, can only send you in return a picture; but the name written on that picture, dear Kate, is that of a Saint. Only fancy, for a fortnight we have had every day Father Hermann here. You have heard of his conversion in 1847, but if you only knew how strongly and continually grace works in his soul, you would join us in thanking God for it. My dear companions are electrified and penetrated by the perfume of his virtues. This good

Father is so fond of our house. He says he finds in it the simplicity of St. Teresa's children. He said Mass for us almost every day, and the children sing his hymns to the Blessed Sacrament with great devotion, which quite delighted him. Yesterday, after writing his name on the little picture I send you, he said, 'Really I have no merit in coming to this house. I feel that Jesus is everywhere in it; in the Blessed Sacrament, in the chapel, in your hearts, in this room, on the stairs, everywhere—in short, I feel that this dear house is impregnated with Jesus and His love.' Our sisters are overflowing with love and gratitude. Do, dear Kate, thank God for all the mercies He vouchsafes to us. This Father's presence has done us great good. One cannot help being the better for coming into contact with his ardent charity. The impressions he leaves behind him are quite peculiar."

Father Hermann felt about Sister Natalie very much as she did with regard to him. He said that in his opinion "she was one of the most beautiful souls in the Church."

Another priest who was capable of appreciating Natalie, who saw her often, and afforded her the support and consolation of his holy friendship, spoke of her as follows: "Sister Natalie," the Abbé de Girardin says, "is one of those nuns whose life is hid in God with Jesus Christ—a perfect type of the Christian virgins who follow the Lamb whithersoever He goes. Her head was generally slightly bowed, her eyes modestly bent down. She had no need to make acts of recollection—God was in her face and in her heart. . . . Her life was a perpetual sermon; and looking at her one understood what St. Francis of Assisi meant when one day he said to one of his monks, 'Let us go out and preach,' and then walked with him through the town in complete silence. They preached by their countenance and example. How often Sister Natalie preached in that way."

In the year 1865, Natalie, by Father Etienne's desire, made another journey out of France. He was going to found a house of Sisters at Gratz, and he took her with him, partly to have her assistance in the work he had in hand, and partly to give the benefit of change of air to her precious and now rapidly failing health.

During her stay at Gratz she had the happiness of seeing her own two sisters, who came from Trieste to spend some days with her. This happiness, and the spiritual joy she felt in the midst of the new foundation, rendered her sojourn at Gratz as delightful as Father Etienne had hoped. Her daily intercourse with this holy Superior of St. Vincent of Paul was an additional grace which made this journey into a pilgrimage full of blessings to her soul, though her health reaped but little advantage from it.

On leaving Gratz, Father Etienne went to Vienna, and there another great and deep joy awaited his travelling companion. She saw there the dear friend who after parting with her had retired to a cloistered convent at so great a distance from her. Natalie's apparition before the grate behind which she found Marie de Bombelles, deeply touched them both. " I was so agitated," Marie said, "with joy and gratitude, that I could hardly speak, and

Natalie's answer to my speechless emotion was her beautiful smile. I thought she looked ill, but when I spoke of my anxiety about her, she said, " Oh, let us leave alone that miserable body; we are going to heaven!"

The change in Natalie was indeed but too evident. As we read her letters, which we shall continue to quote till the end of our narrative, we shall see her ‚from this time forward struggling against the malady which was undermining her life, and becoming every day more painful and distressing. But no complaint ever escaped her lips. Nothing disturbed her thoughts from their habitual course. Suffering seemed to act on her like fire on incense. The sweet beauty of her soul increased under it, and spread around her an atmosphere of holiness. She loved more intensely than ever her poor children, her sisters, her friends, her country,—and God above all and more than all.

We should extend our work too much if we transcribed all the letters written by Sister Natalie during her absence from home. The anxieties of a mother are but a faint image of the care and tenderness which she shows and expresses in this correspondence with regard to all the members of her numerous family. As soon, however, as she found herself once more in the midst of her Sisters, she thought of leaving them again, and perhaps for ever.

The cholera had burst out at St. Petersburgh. The news of its ravages touched a tender chord in Natalie's heart, and she conceived an ardent desire to go and share the dangers of her country people, and to devote herself to the care of the sick in the numerous hospitals hastily organized for their reception. It was on very rare occasions that she expressed any wish of her own, but in this case she asked and obtained leave of her Superiors to act on this impulse. Then, forgetting her bodily weakness, and alas! forgetting also how closed against her were those hearts which she still so faithfully loved, the Russian Sister of Charity ventured to write to the Empress, who was at that time at Nice, and for a few days flattered herself with the hope that her request would be granted, and that she would be permitted to return to her native land to nurse her own people, and die in the midst of them.

But the rarest generosity in the world is that which accepts a sacrifice, and it was not evinced in this instance. The poor Sister's simple and touching letter remained unanswered for three months, and then Count Pierre Schouwaloff wrote civilly but coldly that the epidemic had ceased, and there was no occasion for her services. Not a word of thanks accompanied this reply, the omission of which did not strike Sister Natalie; but she could not but feel the coldness of the reply, and more ardently than ever pined for the day when the icy wall of separation would disappear which divided her, as if she had been guilty of a crime, from those she so earnestly loved.

But in all exterior circumstances she always saw God's will alone, so that these regrets were unaccompanied by depression or discontent. She quietly resumed with unimproved health, and suffering which had become continual, the community life interrupted by her journey. She felt her weakness without complaining of it, and was courageous about everything save the sufferings of her daughters, whom she would have fain relieved from their pains even while she taught them how to bear them, and envied those who died.

Amongst these was one of those creatures whom one cannot help admiring and regretting, like a beautiful vision about to vanish from the earth. Natalie had felt a great sympathy for this young girl ever since she had seen her for the first time and fetched her away from the Mother-house. Her name was Laura. Sister Natalie said to her, "My dear child, will you keep that name in the community? For my part I like it, and would be glad to have a Sister so called in our house." Laura answered, "My name was one of the things I had resolved to sacrifice to God." "Well then," Natalie replied,

"Shall we call you *Agnes?*" The young girl blushed with surprise and pleasure, and thanking her for the choice of that name, said that from her childhood she had always had a peculiar affection for that dear little Saint. And worthily did she bear that sweet appellation;—this young Sister who seemed only just to have appeared amidst her companions to edify them by her holiness, her sufferings, and early death. Like so many others, this pure victim had offered herself up for the salvation of those she loved. But if the sufferings she had asked for were not denied, joy was also bestowed upon her, and that in no ordinary degree.

"Oh! if people only knew," she said in her last moments, "the happiness it is to die a Sister of Charity!" Natalie found her on her return in a hopeless state.

"I envy my Sister Agnes," she wrote, "for I think that she must be pleasing to God; I should like to be as sure of being so myself, and then to die as rapidly. It is sad to grow old on earth when heaven is so beautiful!"

The end was approaching, and the poor Superior had to write to the sister of the dying nun what could no longer be concealed.

"1865. I am commissioned by your little Agnes to tell you secretly that she is getting very weak and cannot last long. She wants you, her sister, to know it, but does not wish you to alarm yet the rest of her family She sends you a little image of St. Joseph; and is holding in her hand one of your patron Saint,—the Blessed Margaret Mary. This picture is like herself, it has the same expression of suffering.

This likeness seems to please her, and as she looked at it she tried to smile. Poor dear lamb! It seems to please our Lord to lead her more and more into a state of complete annihilation. I said nothing about your little invalid; I thought it more prudent not to disturb her perfect peace and calm. She thinks of earthly things only just as much as is necessary. When she speaks of you it is just with a few brief words. It is indeed well that this young flower takes to heaven all its sweet perfume. Our dear Sisters often visit her. She has always a word or a smile for them. Jesus wants and calls her. My very dear M——, should we venture to keep her back if we could?—we who look to the same joys, who await the same happiness?"

A few days later she added, " our dear

Sister Agnes yielded her soul to God yesterday evening, after a short and peaceful agony. The expression of her face was that of a little Saint."

The appearance and the disappearance of this little angel was a sweet though solemn event for Natalie and her Sisters. On the one hand, there was sacrifice, suffering, abnegation, and a young life cut short in its spring-tide; on the other, a prayer answered, a soul saved, an infinite happiness secured after a brief struggle. For those who thought as Natalie did of such events there was more to rejoice than to grieve at in such a death; and it was not wonderful to hear her often exclaim, "I envy my Sister Agnes."

A touching circumstance is related in connection with a little cross — a souvenir and a relic of this angelic young

Sister. She had brought it back from Clamart, where she had been sent for her health, with the intention of giving it to her dear Superior. It was made of the wood of St. Vincent of Paul's oak tree, and was set in silver. When Sister Natalie saw it she said, "Oh, why did you buy it for me?—you know we do not wear silver." Poor Sister Agnes, a little disappointed, said, "But if his Daughters are not to have it, who shall possess this wood from St. Vincent's tree?" Natalie smiled and said, "Well, I accept it, but to give it away." "To one of our Sisters?" Agnes asked, pleased at any rate that her present was not refused. "No, but to your sister as a remembrance both of you and of me."

This precious cross has of course been preserved with love and reverence by those in whose hands it has remained. And it will be no matter of surprise that many a prayer answered, and many a grace vouchsafed, should be connected with it.

We must say a few words more on Natalie's great charity, not only towards missionaries—which she looked upon as her special vocation—but also towards priests in general. She had an intense desire to see noble hearts and devoted souls dedicating their lives to the sacred ministry. It was through their hands that graces were to flow all over the world by means of the Sacraments, and she spared no efforts to remove the exterior obstacles which sometimes stood in the way of their entrance into the Sanctuary. So many are the instances of her zeal in this respect that we cannot relate them all, and must content ourselves with the following account of an occurrence which proved the means of giving to the Church a pious and zealous priest:

Once, when Natalie was in one of the provinces for a foundation, she went to a neighbouring village to visit the good Superior of one of St. Vincent of Paul's houses. She heard there of a young man, who after finishing his studies had been obliged by inevitable circumstances to become a farm servant, though his ardent desire had been to enter the great seminary. Instantly the thought occurred to her of withdrawing from the world a soul on which God seemed to have a special claim. She sought, and soon found, an opportunity of speaking to this young man. On her return to Paris, the following day, it so happened that he drove the carriage which was to take her to the station. On arriving there, she thanked him and said, "Sir, forgive me if I am guilty of an indiscretion; but I have been told that you once wished to be a priest. Have you still the same desire? Should you like to enter the great seminary?" "Sister, your question touches me very much," the young man answered; "my wishes are always the same, I long intensely to be a priest; I see no other way to peace and happiness in this world and in the next; but insurmountable obstacles daily increase. I look upon this wish as a temptation, and I try to drive it away, but in this conflict between my wishes and my fears I can find no rest." "Thank you for those few words," Sister Natalie answered; "I am sorry there is not time for us to converse more at length, for here is the train and I must go. Accept this little picture. Put your trust in God and take courage, and then when you go home promise to write to me a line."

Thanks to Sister Natalie's persevering efforts, all material obstacles were removed. Two years afterwards this young man, after a fervent preparation, entered the great seminary. She had used the most unremitting efforts to this end.

Many similar examples might be quoted of what I am inclined to call Sister Natalie's grand zeal for souls. Without exaggeration, eagerness, or any imprudence, she was always on the look-out for opportunities of assisting others in their spiritual needs, and never allowed a single one to escape her. Her ardent love of God seemed to enlarge her mind as well as to widen her heart.

CHAPTER VIII.

THE only event which from that time until 1870 disturbed Sister Natalie's outward peace, was the death of M. Anatole Demidoff, which happened in Paris, on the 15th of May of that terrible year. She had probably hoped from his great goodness to the poor, and his admiration for a perfect life even under a form which generally excites hostility in those not familiar with it, that he would end by becoming, in a striking and complete manner, a convert to truth and virtue, like so many illustrious persons in other ages and even in our own.

But this was not the case. Natalie was suffered to approach her uncle in his last illness, and they conversed together a great deal. We cannot tell what passed between them. We only know that during all the remainder of her life she always spoke of him with affectionate gratitude, and regrets mingled with much hope. As a Saint has said, "There are depths of mercy between the last sigh of a dying person and God's judgment of the departed soul." May we not feel great consolation when in the scale are thrown the tears and blessings of the poor, the prayers and offerings of holy souls?

During a few months Natalie's illness did not perceptibly increase, and that being the case she was apt to forget its existence and its dangers. It was impossible to induce her to spare her strength

—the children, the poor, the sick, claimed her at every moment, and she never refused to attend to them. The most wretched were those who most attracted her, and in return they showed her a demonstrative affection which would not have been agreeable to people in general. One poor rag-picker, amongst others, made it a point always to embrace her on New Year's Day and on her Feast, which Natalie submitted to in the most gracious manner possible, and did not at all admit that because she was dirty the poor woman was not to kiss her.

She never could make up her mind to send away the children too young to go to school. She used to take charge of them herself. Two of these little creatures were wont to remain whole days by their dear Sister Superior, and were often lying asleep in her room when people came to see her.

She watched over them with the care and patience of a mother, and kept them with her till they were old enough to go into the Orphanage.

The time was gone by when her clumsiness in handling a broom made her unhappy, and amused her Sisters. Just as she excelled in the management of an establishment where there were many people to look after, and very little room, so had she become used to the commonest and roughest work of the house. She took her turn with the others in the business of the kitchen and the laundry, and perhaps the nearest approach to imperfection which was ever detected in Sister Narischkin was her excessive reluctance to give up these fatiguing occupations which taxed her strength too much, long before she would admit it. The Sisters did their best to spare her these labours, but it was difficult to do so consistently with obedience, and even when Sister Natalie had promised to attend to their suggestions on that point, she often found some means or other to have her own way.

Sometimes after a sleepless night spent in coughing the Sisters persuaded her to rest a little, and not to go to the place where she saw and conversed with poor people. But they knew the way to her room, and used to go there straight and to exclaim, "Oh, good Mother, what a joy it is to find you!" Far from sending them away, "Come in, come in," she used to say, "but hide yourselves that the Sisters may not see you." The wish to speak to her was so great that her companions used to try, when they walked with her in the streets, to keep her out of sight, for the moment she was recognized Sister Narischkin was instantly surrounded.

Once when her strength failed her she exclaimed, "Oh, be very self-devoted whilst you are young and healthy!" and then added, "Now that I am ill, always suffering, and of no use, I should be very unhappy but for the consciousness that I did my best as long as I could." One of her companions then ventured to ask her if in former days she had been allowed to perform severe penances. "Oh yes!" she answered simply, "everything I wished for and asked—fasts, hair-cloths, and other instruments of penance." She paused a little, and then said, "I cannot tell you what a consolation it was to me to do those sort of things for our Lord. I spent such happy nights. Now I can do nothing," she added sadly; "but then there is obedience, which supplies for everything else."

Soon after her return, she wrote to her Sister Elisabeth: "Do not those days at our little convent seem to you like a dream? How quickly they elapsed, and how distant they now appear—those rapid moments we spent together. I followed you, in thought, all Friday; but now that you are at Trieste, I don't know where to look for you. I need not tell you how delighted our Sisters were at my return! My only regret was to leave our good Father. The very sight of him gives me the greatest wish to practise every sort of virtue."

TO THE VISCOUNTESS DES CARS.

" The cholera has reappeared at Paris. It pursues its course and there are a great number of deaths. Pray for all the souls which have so suddenly to appear before the judgment-seat of God. If you hear that I am carried away this time, you will I am sure have Masses said for the repose of my poor soul; and you will ask Father Hermann to say Mass for me. Our Lazarist Fathers are all beginning their retreat to-night, so it would not be the moment to choose for leaving this world. But as to that, too, it is better to leave the choice to God. I am sure that you agree with me in that. Oh, yes, always, in everything—without *ifs* and without *buts*—let us unite ourselves in will, in heart, and in mind with Him who is everything and all in all to us!"

After the Emperor of Russia's visit to Paris, in 1867, she wrote to her sisters:

"*July* 14*th*, 1867.

"I am told that well-bred and distinguished people were pleased with the

Emperor, and still more with his second son—the Grand Duke Wladimir.

"On the day after the horrible attempt,* we were ordered to illuminate, like all the other establishments connected with the city of Paris. I felt very keenly, on the occasion of this traitorous attempt, those emotions which people say belong to noble-hearted souls." †

"1868.

"Pray for us on Saturday. It is the great day of the renovation of our vows—those vows which add, each year, a link to the chain which binds us to Jesus. In Passion week I hope, please God, to gain my jubilee, and then will come that other

---

* Berezowsky's attempt to assassinate the Emperor of Russia.

† A famous French Poet says, "À tous les cœurs bien nés, que la Patrie est chère!"

great week so full of increasing emotions that the heart seems unable to contain them.

"You gave me so much pleasure, dear Kate, by telling me the good that 'A Sister's Story' has done to your soul! Pauline also rejoiced to hear it. She came to see me, and we had a long chat together. She has a noble soul, but unfortunately she is over-anxious about events ordained by God's Providence. I should like to see her deeply peaceful!

"Do pray much for our uncle Alexis; he has been much in my mind during all these last days without my knowing why. Now I understand it—as he was needing our prayers. Oh! what a consolation there is in prayer!—of what wonderful efficacy it is in all our temporal and spiritual necessities! . . .

"I am sure, dear Kate, that you do

not forget St. Joseph during this month of March. Pray to him a great deal. He obtains for us what we ask if we beg for it with confidence and fervour; but above all things animate your heart to a great love of Jesus. O Jesus!—life, light, joy, and peace of our souls!—Jesus, our everlasting love! Pray to Him for me, as I always do for you!

" Have you heard of the death of Louise Esterhazy, which happened at Vienna last Saturday? Oh, poor dear Louise!—she would, perhaps, have liked to live on; and I, on the contrary, feel jealous when I see the friends of my childhood taking their departure; I really do not see, if I go on as I am, when I shall ever go!

"I am grieved at a sentence in your letter which shows —— to be so little disinterested. Oh, Kate! what ugly things there are on earth. You are right to say that the only thing to be done is to lift up our eyes to heaven. Let us often do so. There everything is beautiful, encouraging, Divine! Jesus from the midst of His eternal glory calls us to share His bliss, and lavishes upon us His grace for that end. It is, in itself, a priceless gift, and the beginning of the eternal glory He means us to enjoy. Oh, my God!—what good the thought of these great truths does to my soul! I can then rest on Thee with security for my eternal future! Strike as Thou wilt, O Lord, Thou art my Father, infinitely desirous of my happiness. Only make me love Thee, and then do with me what Thou wilt. . . .

"Our good Father Hermann will arrive on Monday. We shall not long enjoy his presence, but it always does one good to see him, for his fervour is constantly increasing. Oh! how sweet it is to love Jesus Christ as the Saints loved Him, and as a multitude of souls love Him even now! This love is such an active and powerful fire that any one filled with it must inevitably communicate its warmth to those around them. I am delighted at the thought of seeing again this fervent religious, if I could only profit a little by his visit!

"Since my dear retreat, instead of being sent to some village in the suburbs to breathe country air, it has been the will of our good God to confine me to my bed, and I see no one. Oh, how delightful it is to abandon oneself to the good pleasure of that merciful Master, in health as in sickness! Everything becomes sweet—too sweet—in His service; and for my part I cannot find that I have the shadow of a wish but that of loving Him, and increasing every day in that love.

"This is also my heart's desire for you, dear Kate. Oh, how I long for the love of Jesus to take possession of your soul and transform your life ! . . .

"Pauline is gone to St. Mars, where they are expecting the remains of her poor brother Fernand. She had never been to that château where Fernand was looking forward to her visit when all the reparations would have been completed; now it is under the present painful circumstances that our Lord has ordained she should go there for the first time. She really seems to be left in this world only to close the eyes of her relatives and mourn over their loss. How all this leads us to the thought of eternity, dear Kate! Yet a little while and our turn will come—sooner, perhaps, than we imagine. For my part, I own that I think of nothing else; I think it does one so much good. It lifts up the heart, and gives the soul such good and fervent desires—for, after all, we shall reap only what we have sown. I send you an emblem which I want you to meditate upon. It reminds one of the happy state of a heart that has died to all things—even itself. It is from this annihilation that a true life springs up, and we must work courageously to obtain it."

We have often met with such words as these elsewhere. They are familiar to the Saints. But good and useful as they are when we read them in their writings, or by hearsay, the impression they make upon us is different when they are connected with personal recollections. It is these recollections, so vividly present in our minds, which give a value in our eyes to each word we transcribe; and if we have at all succeeded in reproducing before our readers the same image, they will, to some degree at least, share our feelings.

We have now arrived at a period when extraordinary and unforeseen events called forth all the energy which our Natalie had gained from constant prayer and union with God. All her remaining strength was about to be spent in a last and courageous effort.

Singularly enough, it was Sister Narischkin who informed her Sister Catherine, then living in a remote part of Austria, of the events that were taking place in Europe, the report of which had not reached her:

"*Paris, July 22nd,* 1870.

"VERY DEAR KATE,

"I was expecting a letter from you, and I see that you are in complete ignorance of what is going on here. May you be in proportion as conversant with the science of the Saints. The world is in a sad state just now. War is declared between France and Prussia; and in the midst of a little of that enthusiasm which always exists when soldiers are about to defend or avenge their country, there are tears shed in abundance. And you have not heard anything of it in your remote corner of Austria? Is this really possible? You do not know also, I suppose, that the small-pox is raging in Paris? Thanks be to God, and the protection of the Sacred Heart always watching over us, our dear house has been preserved from it, but not this locality. We live in a sort of desert. All the hotels are shut up. For every one this is a time of calamity and trial; and the stifling heat produces every sort of illness. The chastisements of Heaven are weighing heavily on the earth. We must redouble the fervour of our daily prayers, of our penances and mortifications.

"What will be the result of this war? God only knows, but in any case it is not a time for you to think of coming to France; this, dear Sister, will, I know, not weigh lightly in the scale of the sacrifices God asks of you. Try to get a little knowledge of what is going on by reading the newspapers. You isolate yourself too much from the rest of the world. I do not like that isolation—it tends to narrow the heart. Now I must leave you that my letter may go to-day. Pray for France, and pray for us. The most terrible news from China has increased our sorrows to the utmost. Eight of our Sisters and one of the Missionaries have been massacred. They are indeed martyrs; but still one cannot help feeling their deaths, especially by means of a despatch which leaves one in ignorance of all details."

Six months later she writes:

"*Paris, February* 13*th*, 1871.

"DEAR SISTER,

"You seem to live in another world, by the surprise you express at not having heard from me. Are you not aware that I am in a town just emerging from a state of siege, and where outward communications are still extremely difficult? We are like lepers, whom everybody runs away from and dreads. I can now really feel with truth that I am dead to the world, and the world more than ever dead to me.

"I wonder at your thinking I can convey your messages to this and that person, when I can hardly find out where all those friends are with whom for six months I have had no communication. If it was not for the sufferings, moral and physical, and the anguish every one endured during the siege, I would for my own part bless those days in which our Lord showed so visibly His care of the children of St. Vincent. No disaster befell any of our houses except such as were purely material. But pray for us, for we are not at the end of our troubles. People are suffering very much in health, in consequence of all the privations they have gone through; and now that provisions are coming in prices are exorbitant. Well, may God help us. We kiss the hand that punishes us, for His chastisements are tokens of mercy."

"*Paris, February* 14*th*, 1871.

"The postal communications are very slow. Everybody complains of it. . . . I sometimes wrote by balloons, but I had not much faith in that mode of correspondence, and am not at all surprised that you did not receive my notes. And then our moral and physical sufferings were so great, that only one want was felt—that of casting ourselves into the Divine Heart of Christ.

"Oh, that happy, happy Father Hermann!* We heard of his death very soon by a letter from Spandau to the Abbé Le Revours. It was on the 28th of January that his beautiful soul took its flight to

---

* He had died at Spandau, on the 28th of January, of typhus fever caught whilst ministering to the sick soldiers.

Heaven. May he obtain for us all a fervent love of Jesus Christ. All is comprised in that. Oh, what a wretched thing life is without that sacred love."

"*March 4th*, 1871.

"I have been intending to write to you for several days, but letters suddenly arrived from every part of the world, and we had to send everywhere tokens of our existence. I longed to tell you what we have heard of the last moments of the saintly Father Hermann. One of our Sisters had the privilege of ministering to him during his illness, and witnessing his end. When he felt that he was dying he asked her if she could sing the 'Te Deum.' 'No, she could not.' 'And the "Salve Regina"?' 'Oh, yes,' she replied. 'Then let us sing it together,' and he began the antiphon with her. As they went on with it, the voice of the dying Saint became weaker and weaker, and then ceased to be heard—he was dead. Oh, what an end, dear sister! If ever I was tempted to the sin of envy, it was from the wish to have been in that privileged Sister's place!

"I have not seen or heard anything of Mademoiselle ——— . . . It is indeed sad to be so often deceived. Alas! it shows that there is nothing good, beautiful, and perfect in this world—Jesus only is beauty, goodness, and perfection itself!

"Our poor Paris is still quite deserted. All sorts of diseases are raging, and people say that it will be for a long time very unhealthy. I have not put my foot out of the house since the 5th of September. My cough is most obstinate, and breaks me to pieces; otherwise I am well."

But the terrible days were now at hand, of which we may well say that "had they not been shortened" she would not have survived them. When, on the 13th of February, she had written, "Pray for us, for we are not at the end of our troubles," her previsions had been but too well-founded. During the awful months of the Commune it was not only the sufferings and material danger which exhausted her remaining strength, but more than anything else the heavy responsibility which weighed upon her.

The anguish of so many important resolutions she had to take, her anxiety for those under her care, and in the end her ardent solicitude for those who—denounced and pursued in every direction—took refuge in the humble house which they looked upon as an assured sanctuary—so great was the popular feeling which guarded it. And God permitted that it should indeed prove such a refuge. But with all her strong faith, its Superior acted under these terrible circumstances according to the laws of that wisdom, human and divine, which teaches to rely absolutely on God, and acts nevertheless as if everything depended on personal exertion. During that time, without for one moment losing her calmness, without any agitation of soul or of manner, she evinced the indomitable energy of her character.

On Holy Tuesday, 1871, she wrote:

"An hour ago they came in great haste to tell me that the mob was pillaging St. Thomas's, and that we ought to shut up the house and hide everything in danger of profanation. Fortunately this has proved a false alarm, but at any moment we may expect these terrible visitors. I hope they will be merciful. The Sacred Heart of our Divine Lord has hitherto protected us in a wonderful manner.

"They have been twice to St. Lazare to look for arms, but otherwise behaved well. At the Val de Grace they visited all the house, from the cellar to the garret, but not the rooms of the Sisters. At other places the mob was furious, and since the fighting has begun they are like madmen. A sort of general terror prevails. If we had not the Divine Heart of our Lord as a shelter, what would become of us? For my own part I feel very peaceful and calm. I do not think anything will happen to us, Jesus is so good.

"Adieu. I send my letter by a good worthy man, who will try to post it at Montlhéry. Our present position is a thousand times worse than during the siege. Pray much for us."

The Sacred Heart!—the Heart of Him who has redeemed us. Is it not a strange thing that these words—the sweetest, the deepest, the most consoling it would seem that human lips can utter—should provoke not only a smile from unbelievers and godless persons, but that many Christians, and even some who call themselves Catholics, do not enter into their meaning, do not feel their beauty. How can this be accounted for? To a certain degree, perhaps, this may be owing to the very imperfect exterior forms this devotion has often assumed—an imperfection partly attributable to the absence, in our days, of high religious art. No Raphael has been found to furnish the world with such a representation of the Divine Heart as he was inspired by faith and Christian genius to give of the mystery of the Holy Eucharist.

But, after all, of what importance are outward forms, even were they everything we could conceive and desire? The great, the real, the only thing that signifies, is the thought they typify. The Cross is the Emblem of the Incarnation. It stands before us as the memorial of the great fact that God became Man, and was crucified for us, and it tells us that we must suffer and die for Him. The Heart is the Emblem of love, and it reminds us that Jesus Christ has loved us, and that we too must and can love Him; that the heart He has given us—that heart which throbs within us when it is moved by strong affection—must beat for Him who made it! To show us the Heart of Christ is to set before our eyes the supreme object towards which our own hearts must gravitate.

I am not addressing these words to infidels, to sceptics, to materialists; I am speaking to Christians—that is, to those who believe that Christ has suffered, has ransomed, and has loved mankind. To such I say, "Did He not die? Did He not rise again? Does He not live for ever, not only as God but as man? Is not our human nature made Divine through Him?—and what is there in nature, what is there on earth more noble—we might almost say more Divine—than the heart's love when the heart is pure?"

What, then, must be the Heart of Him who is the source of all love? Our Saviour said Himself that He had brought fire on earth, and willed it to be kindled. And what is that fire, if not that unchangeable, incomparable love which burns in His Heart, and of which all human affections are more or less faint images, according as that first and supreme love enlightens and inflames them?

This explains, in a few imperfect words, why there are hearts which the very name of "the Heart of Jesus" sets on fire; and such was the case with Sister Natalie. It has been said that the Sacred Heart was her particular devotion. It would be more true to assert that all her devotions, without any exception, arose from that sacred source, and we might add that no real and fervent piety can exist without it. If this is once felt and understood, little attention will be bestowed on the degree of artistic merit in the symbols which represent such an idea; and everything that reminds us of it will be dear to our hearts. This was the case with Natalia. After the Tabernacle nothing in the chapel was as precious to her as the picture which symbolized the love of the Heart of God. But everything there was inexpressibly dear to her, not only as a Holy place, but as the abode of One she tenderly loved. As far as possible she watched herself over each minute detail relating to the Altar, linen, vestments, flowers, and lights, and she maintained everything with the utmost neatness and order. She was also very particular as to her dress and that of her Sisters. The least untidiness seemed to her incompatible with the reverence due to the religious habit.

We can imagine her on the day we are speaking of, alone in that chapel, removing every ornament from it, hiding the sacred vessels and the altar candlesticks,—everything that could tempt the rapacity of the mob; even the gilt frames of the pictures. The one of the Sacred Heart she carried into her own room in order to keep it till the last moment. The lamp, too, she left burning in the little Sanctuary; for she could not make up her mind to have the Blessed Sacrament removed until the danger became imminent and made it necessary to preserve it from sacrilege. During the last days of the struggle some one was always watching on the roof of the house, in order to give timely notice of the approach of the conflagration or the insurgents. Till then she could not bear to leave the Tabernacle empty.

God alone knows what she went through during that melancholy evening in April when she was making these sad preparations. The most fearful rumours reached her, and foreboded the worst; for if the hostages were not yet put to death, they were arrested, and their terrible position kept every one in breathless suspense. It was proposed to increase their number, and horrible threats were uttered which were but too soon realized. Miserable and fatal days!—which seem to belong to some distant phase of history, and which we cannot remember without a shudder — of such recent occurrence too, and yet already half-forgotten by many of us!

Several Lazarist Fathers were amongst the hostages, and, as well as the Jesuits who were arrested at the same time, were only to leave their prison for the scene of their martyrdom. Others were being pursued, and all were in danger. We can easily imagine with what eagerness and self-devotion Sister Natalie received those who successively took refuge in her little convent. During those frightful days she communicated to all around her the peaceful courage which filled her heart. The children had been sent away, to their parents in some cases, or to places of safety out of Paris, but their vacant rooms were filled with persons living in the neighbourhood, who thought that the respect inspired by the house of Charity promised a greater security than they could reckon upon in their own homes. Sister Natalie never refused to admit any one, and shared with these guests the slender resources of the house. Sometimes they were in the most urgent need, and reduced to the strangest expedients in order to find bread. Then came the last awful struggle, and all that made it atrocious, bloody, and infernal.

The troops had entered Paris, but the still unconquered masters of the town were resisting with a desperate rage which vented itself by bloodshed and fire. The burning of the public monuments and the massacre of the hostages seemed the acts of demons rather than men; and, when maddened with fury and drink—after the commission of such deeds—it was plain that nothing could command respect, and no one hoped for mercy.

At that moment the house of the Rue St. Guillaume, surrounded by three barricades, was virtually in the power of the insurgents. One of the most venerated missionaries of the Lazarist community was lying concealed in it since he had been obliged to fly from his own monastery. Fearing that his presence might prove a danger to the Sisters, he was determined at any price to get away, and whatever the danger, to try and reach one of the gates of the town. But Sister Natalie protested against it, and at last consented to his departure only on one condition, and that was that she should accompany him.

The insurgents, even in the midst of their blind fury, still respected the white cornettes which they saw day and night bending over the beds of the sick and wounded and placing their children in safety. Sister Natalie asked leave to cross one of the barricades in order to go to a station, and the permission was granted. She then succeeded in placing in a carriage her venerated guest, and, with another of her Sisters, got into it herself. The two cornettes showed themselves at the windows of the vehicle, and in midst of the fighting and the flames of the burning houses they made their way to the station, and after witnessing the departure of the priest, came home at the end of many weary hours fraught with danger and anxiety to themselves and to the community which welcomed them back at last in safety.

But by that time the extending conflagration was threatening their own house. It did not, however, occur to Natalie to fly. A sort of supernatural confidence, justified by the event, prevented her from feeling frightened; and indeed the news soon reached them that the fire had been extinguished just as it was reaching the wall close to their abode. This danger at an end, all their attention was absorbed in the immediate duties of the moment. Fighting had begun on the barricades, and the wounded combatants had to be tended. These men were Communists; they were shut up together with them within the barricades. They nursed them as devotedly as if they had been their best friends. One may almost add that they became such; for we are bound to place it on record that during this strange time of communication between the Sisters and the insurgents, neither of the parties had the least complaint to make against the other.

Alas! poor deluded people! Excited by hard, proud men—against those who really love them, belong to them, and suffer with them and for them—their wild madness is more a subject for prayer than for wrath and condemnation.

May the blood of the victims, and their pleadings for their murderers, obtain for the insane, recovery; for the guilty, remorse; and for the next generation all that ours is purchasing at so dear a price—the reign of order—in peace, in concord, and in truth!

CHAPTER IX.

1871.

THE struggle once ended, after a brief moment of stupor France began to breathe again, and the throbbings of her vigorous life to reassume their vitality. So little was it affected by events which for other nations would have proved fatal convulsions, that there is reason to be astonished and grieved at the rapidity with which these awful occurrences seem to pass away from our memories!

But in Sister Natalie's soul they had left traces of most painful emotion. After the dangers which she had met with such dauntless bravery were over, a strong reaction ensued. The bloody pavement of Paris seemed, she said, to burn her feet; the smell of petroleum to poison the air, and to follow her wherever she went; but above all, the sufferings, the crimes, the calamities, the offences against God and man she had witnessed, filled her soul with horror, and incessantly haunted her. For one so overflowing with love of God and charity to her neighbour, this was a real martyrdom. Her overwrought nerves absolutely required rest, and a change of air and scene.

Her Superiors perceived this, and sent her to spend a month at Dax, near the tomb of St. Vincent of Paul. And so far as her nerves went, and her peace of mind, the required result was completely obtained. But as to her physical strength, neither rest nor remedies could ever again restore it, and it was only her indomitable energy that prolonged a struggle the end of which was evidently neither uncertain nor distant.

From the time of her return she almost continually had to keep her bed. The fluctuations in her state occasionally brought with them a few days of comparative ease, which she instantly took advantage of to resume her community life. It was only quite at last, and when completely prostrated by illness, that she was induced to give up entirely the exterior and active duties of her post. As to other obligations, she never omitted them. To the very end she went on occupying herself with the spiritual and material direction of the community intrusted to her, and it was only on the eve of her death that she ceased to watch over the administration of the house.

The shortness of her letters shows us how such efforts must have taxed her energy. We find in them evidence of increasing suffering, increasing weakness, and ever-increasing fervour. She wrote on the 23rd of February, 1873, to the Viscountess Des Cars, who had just lost her mother:

"I deeply sympathize with your grief. You can rely upon my poor prayers and those of my Sisters for that dear soul—dear to us on so many accounts. . . . You are coming out of retreat, your heart well prepared for so great a sacrifice. And then Jesus, your beloved Lord, is there to strengthen you. Oh, blessed are the hearts which belong to God!"

Some days afterwards she adds:

"Oh, all that you tell me is very true and very consoling! What a difference between what we see and we look forward to! What a delightful surprise for the soul! What overwhelming joy!"

But according to her own desires she seemed to be too slowly drawing near the end. In a letter dated April 28th, 1873, which she could not finish, we find these words:

"I must leave off. I am spitting blood again, and my cough is most obstinate. Still I dare not hope to go soon to heaven. Let it be when our Lord wills it. For one moment I flattered myself that the hour was come, but the hope proved fallacious."

This time she was mistaken. That blood-spitting was indeed the signal of the instant so ardently longed for. Soon

Natalie perceived it by the increasing and absolute debility which was to be the last phase of her long suffering. Not to be able to speak or move without a great effort was no longer to live, and yet it was not death. This was her greatest trial, but like all others she endured it peacefully. Her poor companions understood that this sudden prostration of powers, which had hitherto maintained themselves amidst the severest attacks of her illness, were a token of the approaching end, and could not conceal from her their affliction. "Do not make yourselves so unhappy," she said to them. "After all, I cannot stay for ever with you. I really must go to Heaven, and you will follow me."

Patience, submission, perfect resignation to God's will, give the strength to endure suffering, but they do not deliver us from it. On the contrary, these virtues are called into action by the most acute pains. Natalie not only had to bear a prostrating exhaustion, but also a severe cough, with frequent blood-spittings, paroxysms of suffocation, and a complete loss of sleep and appetite.

She did not disguise her ailments. She accepted remedies, thanked those who watched over her, and became every day more gentle, more calm, more serene. She begged her Sisters not to pray for her recovery, but for the grace of a perfect patience. One of them said that she was going to ask our Lord to relieve her dear Mother from her sufferings, and to give them to herself instead. Natalie smiled, and answered:

"And do you really think I would make them over to you? You are quite mistaken; I am not so generous as that."

Once when she was struggling in one of her violent fits of coughing, which seemed to tear her to pieces, some one said, "Oh, that dreadful cough!" "No," Natalie replied, "do not call it dreadful, I have bargained with our Lord that each fit of coughing will stand for an act of love."

When her Sisters said, as they took leave of her for the night, that they hoped it would be a good one, she replied, "It will be as God chooses;" or else, "I hope it will be a good one in His sight. May the will of God be done; I will all He wills —to lie awake or to sleep, to suffer or to get well, to live or to die, comes to the same for me; I will not, I cannot, now ask for one thing rather than another."

Such were the words which escaped her lips whilst under the pressure of suffering. During her sleepless nights it was the thought of Purgatory which chiefly occupied her mind. "Oh, how shall we ever bear the privation of the beauty of God after having once seen Him, and yet it will be a blessing to be in Purgatory. But pray that it may not be for a long time." She often dwelt on that subject. "I do implore of you," she said, "not to go and say that I am good, and call me a Saint when I am dead. Pray for me a great deal, and get others to pray."

When, towards the end of her life, she suffered from fever, "I am burning," she would say; "Oh that it were with the love of God!" "Yes," her companions answered, "it is indeed with that love your heart is burning." "No," she replied, "I am too great a wretch for that, but I only wish it was so."

It pained her to give trouble in the night to the Sister who was taking care of her, and as long as she could possibly do without her assistance she used to cry out, "I forbid you to rise." When suffering or suffocation obliged her to sit up, she moved as noiselessly as possible in order not to awake her.

"I offered, one night, to replace her in her bed," this Sister wrote, "and lifted her up in my arms for that purpose. The next day she asked me, in a very serious and earnest manner, if it had not tired me, adding, 'It was a great relief to me.' You may imagine my answer, and with what happiness I carried her ever since backwards and forwards from her bed to her arm-chair. Three of us used to sit up with her in turn. Oh, I was so happy to do something for her, and that she allowed me to nurse her. I enjoyed this happiness for a month. It was too great a one for me. Our Lord required the sacrifice of this joy. He sent me an illness which laid me up in the infirmary, and I could not wait upon her any more. It was all over—she had died by the time I got well."

Far more than her sufferings she minded the necessity of obeying the physicians, who insisted on her having better and more delicate food than the community was in the habit of using. For a long time she objected to the least difference being made in this respect, and as long as she could crawl to the refectory it was impossible to persuade her to eat different food to the rest of the community.

Sometimes when they provided for her

some little dainties, such as fresh vegetables or early fruit, and said they were not as dear as she supposed, she would answer, "In that case get some for all the Sisters, not for me alone." She used to make over to her neighbour at table what had been prepared for her. The poor Sister who cooked for the community was often puzzled between her wish to obey the doctor and the fear of disobeying her Superior or deceiving her. Natalie used to detect her little tricks, and refused to avail herself of their result.

What troubled her most during her illness was the thought of increasing the expenses of the house, and she would have been really anxious on the subject if this difficulty had not been solved in an unexpected manner. We see this in the following letter:

"I should be very glad if —— (one of her relatives who was then in Paris) could help me a little to relieve the community of all the expenses entailed upon it by my illness, for the Sisters go through many privations in order to provide me with good food and other comforts. If she is kindhearted I think she would do so. This is the only trial, of illness in a house of charity,—although nothing can exceed the good-will of the Sisters, who never seem to think there is the least difficulty about it. The poor Superior, who knows better than any one else the poverty of the community, is quite aware that without great sacrifices her poor companions cannot provide for her all the doctor orders—chicken, good broth, and other things which we are never in the habit of eating."

On this account she resisted everything

done for her out of the common way. But when she became so weak that it was impossible for her to leave the infirmary, or to digest the only kind of nourishment she would allow to be procured, her last days would have been shortened, perhaps, had her orders been obeyed,—or her peace of mind troubled had they been transgressed,—but for the sudden thought of a kind friend whose affection was ever on the watch.

This was that Countess N——, who was in the habit of coming to Paris every year to see her. She was living at a distance, and ill herself, just at the moment when she would most have wished to be near Natalie. Every day, and sometimes more than once a day, she received tidings of her health, guessed what nobody said or suspected, and wrote to a M. Rouzé, who kept a café in the Rue St. Dominique, begging him to send daily to the convent whatever delicacies the doctor ordered for Sister Narischkin. This good man had, she knew, a perfect veneration for the holy Sister of Charity, and he did acquit himself of the commission entrusted to him with the greatest zeal and care.

Natalie humbly accepted as alms the things which were thus sent to her, and thanks to her friend's thoughtful generosity her strength somewhat revived. A few days more of that precious life were vouchsafed to those who saw her with anguish drawing near to her end. This opportune assistance delivered her from a painful anxiety, and gave her physical strength to speak, and to pray up to the last moment.

The most sensible of her privations was the impossibility of going down to the chapel for Mass; but she would not, as was suggested to her, apply for permission from the Nuncio to have Mass said in her room.

"No," she answered, "when God sends us illness we must accept the sacrifices attached to it." "Oh, dear Mother!" one of her companions exclaimed when she was in one of her paroxysms of suffocation, "how I wish I was a Saint!" "What would you do then?" "I would perform a miracle, and cure you!" "But, my good Sister, it is not, you see, God's will I should be cured," Natalie quietly replied.

One day, when she was more exhausted than usual, a Sister from a distance paid her a visit, and said, "It must be very sad for you not to be able to govern your community as usual." Natalie smiled and made no reply, but when the visitor was gone she said to her companions, "It was a funny remark. If it is our Lord's will I should be ill, it would be a pretty thing indeed for me to wish for anything else!"

In the spring of 1874, the last of her life, she heard of the illness and death of her venerable Superior, Father Etienne. This was one of the greatest afflictions which could have befallen her; but she felt so sure of soon following him that she listened to all the details of his edifying end with a calm resignation, which at another time would have cost her great effort. She felt nearer to those friends who had preceded her to heaven than to those she was leaving behind her on earth.

Her sister Catherine continually occupied her thoughts during the last months of her life. She had met with a severe accident, and was still suffering from its consequences. Natalie seemed to feel much more intensely her sister's pains than her own, and kept praying and offering up all her sufferings for her.

The close of this holy life was, however, approaching. One evening, towards the end of July, 1874, she said, "Dear Sisters, help me to die well. We can only die once;" and then pressing the crucifix to her lips, she exclaimed, "Oh, pray a great deal, and get many prayers for me, I entreat you; do not let me languish long in Purgatory."

Her constant fever, her weakness, her sleepless nights, did not for a single instant affect her serenity or the clearness of her mind. The doctor was astonished at it, and said this was scarcely ever the case in such an illness! "What a rare, beautiful organisation!" he exclaimed; and indeed the most perfect harmony reigned between this pure soul, this superior mind, and that subdued and obedient body, the sufferings of which she held as nothing. In the midst of the throes of a mortal disease which consumes by degrees all the vital powers, and only deals its last blow when all has been destroyed, she persevered not only in the accomplishment of every possible act of piety, but continued to attend to the government of her community. On the Saturday before her death she made up, as usual, the weekly accounts; and as she laid down her pen said, "I think this is for the last time."

On the 2nd of August her condition became more critical. She received the last Sacraments, and in the afternoon it was for the first time supposed that she was light-headed. She spoke with some agitation of a sum of money which was missing, and imagined it was mislaid in her bed. But after a further search the money was found, and it turned out that she was quite in her right senses, and had not been anxious without reason. That day she said, looking on the side of her bed, "Oh, what a beautiful child that is!" Whether this was a vision, or a dream, or an hallucination, we cannot pretend to say. Nothing led to the belief that her faculties were in the least impaired. All that night and the following day she spoke as sensibly, as simply, and as humbly as usual, begged pardon of her companions for whatever she might have done to grieve them, thanked them all for their care of her, and with a touching solicitude, thought of every one of them individually.

On that day Father Gagarin—a Russian convert, and a Religious like herself—came to see her for the last time. Her face was so pale and transparent that she seemed no longer to belong to earth. On her brow there was a Divine peace. She was very glad to see him, and spoke in her usual manner, and with her accustomed extraordinary forgetfulness of self, not a word did she say of her own sufferings, but a great deal of those he was enduring, and which made him almost unable to walk. Those two souls sympathised in their ardent love for Russia—their common country. It was right that by the side of Natalie's death-bed should kneel a representative of that Fatherland she so much loved. Well may it be said of her, that in imitation of our Divine Lord, " She loved her own, and loved them to the end."

Up to that time she had been consoled and assisted by M. l'Abbé Ramailhe, curé of St. Thomas D'Aquin, her own pastor and confessor, who had been better able than any one to appreciate the beneficial effects produced on all around her by the holy Sister about to die. Obliged by an imperative duty to leave her after the administration of the last Sacraments, and afraid he might never see her again, he pressed his lips on her dying hand, thus paying her beforehand, as he himself said, the homage due to the relics of Saints.

In the evening of the 4th, an unexpected consolation was vouchsafed to Natalie. The Holy Father's special blessing was brought to her by the Apostolic Nuncio. It was worded as follows:

"The Holy Father blesses the sick Sister, and prays that our Lord may give her perfect resignation, and all the consolations which she needs."

Natalie listened with clasped hands, and evident emotion and joy, to the august and paternal message thus conveyed to her. She begged to hear it read several times, and pressed the paper to her lips. On the night of the 4th, to the 5th, a severe paroxysm seemed to presage a speedy end; but she rallied again, and at four o'clock asked for water in order to wash before receiving the Blessed Eucharist, which since she had been in great danger was brought to her every day.

It was on the 5th of August, at five o'clock in the morning, that she received Holy Communion for the last time on earth.

At seven, another and still more severe paroxysm took place, and the Rev. Father

Chinchon, whose guidance and example had so powerfully assisted her to rise to a high perfection, was by her side at that moment to support and conduct her to the last solemn and blessed close of her life.

When he arrived Sister Natalie was asked if she wished to see him alone. She turned to him with a smile and said, "I have nothing more to tell you, Father." He said he would go and pray for her in the chapel. "Thank you," she said, "it will give me great pleasure." He went, but soon returned. When she saw him again, "Oh! Father," she exclaimed, "are you there? This is still an earthly consolation;" and then, with the humility which to the last moment never forsook her, added, "but I am taking up too much of your time; I am not worth it." Again she asked to hear the Holy Father's words of blessing, clasped her hands together, and did not speak any more; but the expression of her countenance, as she looked at her Sisters, seemed to say, " We shall meet again in heaven; pray for me." They were all surrounding her bed, and began to recite the last prayers. . . . Before they were ended her happy soul had taken flight, and before the eyes of her poor companions there only remained her inanimate form; but on her forehead and her lips there was impressed the stamp of that heavenly bliss which was beginning for their Mother !

We cannot attempt to describe the universal desolation produced by the fatal news when it became known in Paris. It has been seen what her Sisters and her children and her poor people felt for her, but we have not, perhaps, sufficiently dwelt on the veneration she inspired to all her neighbours, to the clergy of her parish, and all that world of charity in Paris—that great world, in the right sense of the words—in which there was no heart that did not ache at the news of her death. It was as if a heavenly vision had disappeared, as if a guardian angel had vanished from sight. Every one called to mind what a blessing her presence amongst them had been, and wondered how her loss could be supplied. Better than any words of her own could do, a letter written by one of her companions in the first hours of bereavement will show us what were the feelings of that poor little community, deprived of its loved Mother. It is written by the Sister who had nursed Natalie with such intense joy and self-devotion, but having herself fallen dangerously ill had never had the happiness of seeing her again alive. She embraced her, however, after her death, and for two days could gaze upon her mortal remains.

The following words were addressed to the faithful and loving friend who, from a distance, had so fondly provided for Natalie's wants during her illness:

"During the two days that she remained in the large room her face was so calm that it seemed to express the happiness of her departed soul. She was dressed in her habit and her cornette, and covered with flowers and garlands. A number of persons came to visit her remains, many of whom remained the whole night. It seemed so difficult to leave. Rosaries and other pious souvenirs were made to touch her body; a number of white nosegays were laid at the foot of her bed."

"On Thursday, Father Chinchon came to pray by the side of her whom in life he had so much helped to attain the place in heaven she now enjoys. He was very much overcome."

"*Friday, August 7th.*

"At nine o'clock she was laid in her coffin. I shall never forget how beautiful she looked. We think that God permitted this transformation. There was a bloom on her cheeks. Her hands and her whole body were soft and pliable. She had never in life looked so lovely. She reminded us of those images of holy martyrs which are seen in Rome. Her attitude was similar—the hands crossed over each other, and her knees covered with a sheet, where a quantity of flowers were thrown. I give you all these details in order that you may picture to yourself her beauty. It was something wonderful. We could not help feeling that we were looking at a Saint. But at last the moment came to take a final leave of her, to give her a last kiss. The Sisters carried her down and placed her in the mortuary carriage of the poor. Our good curé was absent, but everything was done to honour the memory of our Mother. Good Father Chinchon was there, with a great number of Lazarist Fathers. The crowd was immense. The Mayor and the Rev. Father Mailly accompanied the body to the grave. The Sisters and the poor people followed. I felt very sad at that moment, for I was too weak to walk from the church to the cemetery, and was obliged to go home; but good Madame H— called for me in her carriage, and drove me to the burial-place of that dear one to whom I owe everything. Father Gagarin was there. When the remains of the Mother we loved so much were consigned to the grave, our good Father stood at the head of it, with M. Mailly, M. l'Abbé Rivié, and many others. She was laid at his feet, and he remained there all the time. What were his thoughts at that moment with regard to the soul that was so dear to him? No doubt he was offering prayers for her, which will have gone straight to the Heart of our Lord Jesus Christ. We must nevertheless go on praying for her. She used so often to say to us, 'I beseech you do not say, "She was good, she was holy," but pray for me.' I write all this to enable you to picture to yourself everything; but I add no comments. They would not be equal to your own thoughts on the subject.

"No one has been appointed in her place. An assistant Sister came to spend the day here. She was very kind to us, and said, 'Do not expect to find another like her, for such a one does not exist.' People at Paris can talk of nothing else. Though she saw so few persons, the beauty of her soul was well known, and the perfume of her virtues seems to have penetrated everywhere. Do you not feel now as if our Mother was nearer to you than before?—that she, as it were, surrounds you?—and that instead of writing, you can speak to her, that she hears you and can help you? I think she must have become a second guardian angel for one she loved so much, and who during her severe sufferings procured her so much relief. For my part, I cannot rise above my wretched nature, and I feel to miss her terribly."

She was buried in the Mont Parnasse Cemetery, in the enclosure reserved for the

Sisters of Charity. But as this space is, alas! too small to enable them all to remain there, Natalie's family and friends obtained leave to transport her—some time afterwards—to a separate tomb. They chose a spot, the nearest they could find to the Sisters' Cemetery. A little white marble monument, surmounted by a Greek Cross, marks the place where Sister Natalie rests. Often and often people kneel before her tomb, and bring flowers and garlands to adorn it. And we can say, as did one of the keepers of the cemetery, on the day when an immense crowd of Parisians of every rank followed with tears her humble funeral, "Oh, how good that Sister must have been, to make people love her so much!"

Such was Natalie Narischkin from her childhood to her last day. Her life was like one of those musical strains, true and harmonious from the first, weak at the outset, which go on increasing, deepening, and rising evermore in tone and in melody, until they have stirred the heart, and filled the whole atmosphere with their pervading sweetness.

But that other strain, more beautiful than any earthly one, "more worthy of homage than even the voice of genius"—that Divine melody which emanates from a holy soul—will the faintest echo of that Divine music be found in these pages? Will they console and rejoice some of those who were acquainted with Sister Natalie, and who knew the beauty of her soul? Will they make others appreciate her? Will they lead her kindred to exult in the holy fame she has attached to their name, and the land of her birth, which she so much loved, to venerate her memory? We dare not trust that such will be the result of our labours, for a sense of our deficiencies never struck us more forcibly than now when we have brought them to a close. But we venture to indulge that hope, for we have asked God to bless our work, and on Him alone we rely.

THE END.

BY THE SAME AUTHOR

A SISTER'S STORY

FROM THE FRENCH OF
MRS. AUGUSTUS CRAVEN

BY
EMILY BOWLES

The Popular Edition

In one volume, crown 8vo, Cloth, price Six Shillings

LONDON
RICHARD BENTLEY AND SON
Publishers in Ordinary to Her Majesty the Queen
1877

www.ingramcontent.com/pod-product-compliance
Lightning Source LLC
Chambersburg PA
CBHW030820230426
43667CB00008B/1301